THE ANTIDOTE
TO PREJUDICE

THE COLLECTED POEMS
OF
MOIRA BAILIS

VOLUME I

DAVID MESSINEO, EDITOR

The Poet's
Press
PITTSBURGH, PA

Rev 1.2, 2017

This is the 190th publication of
THE POET'S PRESS
2209 Murray Avenue #3
Pittsburgh, PA 15217
www.poetspress.org

This book is also published as a PDF Ebook.

ISBN 0-922558-52-3 (paperback)
ISBN 0-92258-53-1 (hardcover)

TABLE OF CONTENTS

PRELUDE: A CHILD DREAMS OF TRAVEL

A Time for Dreaming   3
Our Easy Talk   4
Fifteen   5
Drawing   6

TO IRELAND IN THE FADING TIMES

Holy Ground Rifearta   9
Mo Theanga   10
Sharavogue   11
Lough Dan   12
Boys Swim   13
Winter Comfort   14
Tinkers   16
Stiles   17
Sunday Afternoons in Ireland   18
Brambles in Ireland   19
I Have Been to Ballylee   20
On Seeing Maud Gonne, Dublin 1942   21
Neutral Territory   22
Antinomian Age   23
Emergency   24
Icarus 1944   25
The Hero   26
Latest Fad   27
I Do Miss the Sea   28
Table Manners (Early Version)   29
Ancestors   30
Burning Coal   32
Abandoned Ceremonies   34
The Last Tram, November 1949   35
Savoirse   36
Nineteen Fifty-Seven   37
Patrick Kavanagh on Pembroke Road   38
Mass Day in the Church at Dalkey   40
Poem on Visiting Bowers Court   41
Summer Evening at New Street   42
Achill   43
To Sheelagh Kirby   44
Roan Inish   45
Nanny   46

Letter from Ireland 48
Green Walk Above White Rock 49
At Shannon Park 50
Going Back 51
The Park 52
The Seat at Saval Park 53
Bisque 54
Prayer 55
Friend (At the Bay) 56
Lost Loves 58
An Old Place 59
Remembering Killiney Bay 60
Killiney 62
At Killiney Bay 64
Continuum 65
Three Rock Mountain 66
On Hearing the Baily Will Lose Its Light Keeper 67
The Secret at the Heart of the Rose 68
Dún Laoghaire 69
Irish Summer 70
A Backward Look 71
Stone from Rifearta 72
Sea Change 73
Endless Change 74
Ireland Unseen 75
Alternate Lifestyle 76

EUROPE IN AND AFTER WWII

9 Sept 1939 79
Wir hatten uns gefürchtet... 80
Teddy Bear Coat 81
Buckingham Palace 83
The Day I Sang to Cows 84
The Lions of Rome 85
The City Astonishing 86

EURASIAN INFLUENCE

Soldier's Tale 1955 89
Xristos Voskres 90
Hymn for America 91
Laika 92
Indo-China (June 26, 1972) 93
Vietnam Christmas '67 94

Vietnam Christmas 1969   96
In China   97

AUSTRALIA REMEMBERED
Outback   101

ANTARCTIC BLAST
Snowfall   105

A IS FOR AFRICA
A Is for Aardvark   109
Practice Run for Africa   110

SOUTH OF OUR BORDER
Sol   113
Pearls in Pink Cups   114
Summer Storm   115
Tocsin at Waslala, Nicaragua   116
Monarchs   117

CROSSING CANADA AND AMERICA
Reading the Weather   121
Sighting Land   123
Wood   124
South Rim   125
Coming from Fort Worth   126
Crossing the Des Moines in Autumn   127
Winterset   128
Winterset Revisited   129
Thinking About Minneapolis   130
Heartland   131
Mississippi Death Trip   132
The Museum at Cullowhee   134
Heritage   135
Spillway   136
Fontana   137
Fiddle Music   138
Cherokee Poet   140
Antietam   141
Grosse Île   142
Dreamers   144
Akewesasne   146

The Loss of the *Dorchester*, February 1943   147
The Farm at Derry   148
At Frost's Grave   150
Wreath from Vermont   151
Lake Tear of the Clouds   152
Diner   153
Sense of Place   154
Retreat   155
Vision Quest   156
Upstate   157
Tappan Zee   158
George Washington, If You Could See Your Bridge   159
The Diadems of the Hudson   160
Aftermath   161
NY Man   162
Moment in Midtown   163
New York City   164
Miss Holybrooke in Central Park   165
Mr. Meyer at Coney Island   166

JERSEY TRAILS

Aug 2005 — Riegelsville, PA   171
Highlands   172
A Jersey Welcome   173
Sept 22 — Sussex Branch, Augusta to Branchville   174
The Paulinskill Valley Trail   176
Waiting for Stef in Blairstown   177
Hiking the Lockwood Gorge   178
Hiking the Columbia Trail   179
Clinton Furnace (Early Version)   180
Clinton Furnace   181
Autumn Rapture — Clinton, NJ   182
Jersey Day   183
Ballooning   184
Hunterdon Blackberry   185
Fragment of a Villanelle   186
Hiking the Old Lackawanna   187
A Meaning Beyond Expected Explanations   188
A Peaceful Place   189
Jersey Shore (A Thought)   190
The Source   191
New Bridge   192
Hackensack   193

Ghosts   194
At the Steuben House   195
Cemetery Trio   196
Looking for Pop's Grave   198
Gulls in Little Ferry   199
Hudson   200

FORT LEE JOURNEYS

Winter Stroll, Fort Lee   203
Main Street, Fort Lee   203
At the Diner   204
Irish Voices   205
Ordinary Noises   206
Four Haiku   207
Hero   208
Alone in the Cemetery   21109
Tohmey   210
The Church on the Hill   212
Tonight   212
Shadows   213
The Eve of Christmas   214
Simplicity   215
The Bike   216
Walking — A Prose Poem   217
To an Irish Friend   218
No Words Suffice   220
New House   221
Mornings on Abbott   222
Ode   223
Chair Mirror Window Sky   224
Nail   225
Cleaning House   226
Back Yard   227
Habitat   228
Dandelion   229
Creeper   230

CODA: THE ANTIDOTE TO PREJUDICE

Righteous People   233

AFTERWORD AND NOTES

Afterword by David Messineo   235

About Moira Bailis   238

The Travels of Moira Bailis, 1921-2011
    by Stefan Bailis   242

Publication Credits — America and Ireland   244

Poem Titles Excluded from This Compilation   253

About the Editor   255

About This Book   257

Prelude:
A Child Dreams of Travel

A Time for Dreaming

From the windows we saw
the racing waves of the sea
crash on the rocks on the coast.
The wind hurled itself against
our house,
howled down the chimneys,
blew gusts of smoke into
the rooms
where we sat, reading
Time and *Life,*
imagining the sun
on Miami Beach
and all the fun everyone
in those glossy colored pictures
seemed to be having.
It was a time for dreaming.
Lamps lit at 4 o'clock
those short winter days —
sundown at four o'clock,
the sky over the distant city
a blue-gray haze
from the thousand coal fires
and on the air in the
country
the reek of peat smoke.
My father would say
"The glass is low"
tapping the old barometer
in the long, dark hall
on the sitting room wall.

<3>

Our Easy Talk

Our easy talk
of everyday things
rises and falls
in the shadowy room.
Outside the evening light
fades behind the trees.

Each moment
has its own special flavor.
You tell me stories
of what it was like
to be young
in New York.

A world away
I listen
trying to imagine a city
that, now, is like a foreign country.

<4>

Fifteen

We sailed up the Shannon
from Athlone to Longford
and the moon shone
over the fens of Roscommon
and cast a patch of
light over the water
and I was fifteen and
in simple joy, took hold
of the moment and
remembered it forever.

<5>

Drawing

I wanted to see the place
I lived in
so I got a big sheet
of white paper
and started drawing.

First I drew a wiggly line
the coast along
the Irish Sea
then I drew the great
granite piers
at Dún Laoghaire
and the hills above
the town —
that was easy,
just three wavy lines.

But, after I had put
our house at the
top of Saval Park
and Killiney Castle above it,
my pen began to falter.

I thought of all the
houses in the neighborhood
and how many roofs
and gardens I would
have to draw.

So, I decided, daydreaming
about flying like a sea gull
over the landscape
was the better way
to know where I was —

<6>

To Ireland
In the Fading Times

Holy Ground Rifearta[1]

It is filled with spirits.
The very air seems to vibrate
with inhalations and exhalations
down the centuries.

Why did they abandon it?
Were they ashamed of its simplicity
the humble structure in the woods
a sanctuary of the poor?

To go there now is to feel
sanctified —
all around the whispering of
the trees
its little window opening
out into the woods
its heavy entry
opening on peace and tranquility
its interior open to the weather
moss and lichen on its
thousand-year-old stones.
How simple it is to
pray there
surrounded by shadows
of Wicklow people long gone
who worshipped here.

---

[1] *Rifearta*. Ruins of a small church located in Glendalough, a Viking-era monastic settlement.

<9>

Mo Theanga[2]

What stifled this tongue,
nearly killed it?
Smothering it
as it sought a way out
from the cemetery of language.

Constrained, it tried
to mimic itself
in mBearla [3]—
became an object of
derision.

It struggled
to make itself heard
over the windstorm
that failed to
silence it.

I find a compromise —
sign posts,
a few places,
Ros Muc, Droichead Nua,
children's names,
and letters beginning
"A Chara."[4]

---

[2] *Mo Theanga.* My language (Irish Gaelic).
[3] *mBearla.* English (Irish Gaelic)
[4] *A Chara.* My dear (Irish Gaelic)

<10>

Sharavogue

I remember the sunlight coming
through the half-opened window
outside the gardens, empty in the June sunlight
while a nun, in black habit and
white coif
taught us about the Fir Domnann
and the Tuatha de Danann[5]

I was bored —

Now I wish I could recall
her simple lesson
on the long-lost history
of the early people
in my country.

---

[5] *Fir Domnann* and *Tuatha de Danann*. Legendary early inhabitants/invaders of
Ireland, attributed with magical powers

<11>

Lough Dan

He could not bear
the beauty
of his world
asked to become
part of it
to be enfolded
in the embrace
of the earth
the rugged land
all mountains
lakes and valleys
a swoon in his
heart
as he stood
above Lough Dan
he was consumed
by beauty[6]

---

[6] This poem is about Moira's brother Jim, a naturalist who lived his last year or
so above Lough Dan.

<12>

Boys Swim

where the
rushing stream
tumbles into
the glen
boys swim
the sound of
their shouts
only in sense
different to
the rivers
hurrying on
the mules with
the skips

<13>

Winter Comfort

*In memory of Welsh miners
of the Nineteen-Thirties.*

Years ago, in Winter's chill
I sat by the hearth.
Outside, roaring winds
fresh from the Irish Sea
rushed about the house,
howling as if protesting
the world's agonies.

I listened to the crackle
of burning coal.
Sometimes a blue flame,
a hiss, a sound
as if a pleading voice
cried out in pain —
I thought of the miners.

Those men of the Thirties
wearing caps and scarves,
their faces seamed with coal dust,
digging, digging, digging
back-breaking shifts
in stifling caverns.
Hewers of "Black Diamonds."

When disaster struck
I saw pictures,
wives and mothers and
weeping children,
clinging together
at the pit-head.
What price my Winter comfort?

<14>

Through the cold season
I thought of those Welshmen
walking from the pits
singing chapel songs,
their voices deep and haunting.
And carrying caged canaries
the color of Spring daffodils
in the Rhonnda Valley.

<15>

Tinkers[7]

I remember
at a bend in the road,
grassy, half-enclosed
by a stone wall —
they would pitch tent.
I would walk by
with my brothers,
smell the acrid scent
of old fires, long doused,
old clothes
on the bushes.
A few rags
would flutter.
A few days later
only the burnt
circle in the grass
would tell that they
were there.

---

[7] *Tinkers*. A nomadic class of people, similar in lifestyle to Romana ("Gypsies") but of different ethnicity. They made their living mainly from repairing metal products, and their nickname derives from "tinsmith."

<16>

Stiles

Once stiles made you welcome
announced a right-of-way
to fields starred with daisies
and woods where violets grew.
The best ones were
three stone steps
set into a wall
smoothed over the years
by footsteps of country folk.
Stiles were a two-way compact
between the walker and the farmer;
no one trespassed
where there were stiles,
all that was asked was —
be gentle with the land.
That is how it was
in the country long ago.

They don't build stiles anymore
in stone walls.
These days there are gates,
padlocked.

<17>

Sunday Afternoons in Ireland

When I was a child
people walked those three hills
on frosty winter afternoons
or, when the weather was mild,
their dogs bounding beside them
they climbed to the obelisk
and sat,
their faces touched by the sun,
the south wind from
the mountains.
For hour on hour
every Sunday it was
a common sight
to see the line of cars
parked on the Vico,
the nature gazing
at the blue mountains
and the glassy sea.

<18>

Brambles in Ireland

On a country road in Ireland
my cousin picks blackberries
from the rain-drenched hedges,
her fingers stained purple,
drops of rain on her hair.
The dewy berries drop one by one
into her silver can,
sustenance for the windy days
of gray winter weather.

Tonight stewing berries
will scent her kitchen
with the captured
fragrance of September.
In the dark afternoons
of the low sun season,
as she takes tea by the fire,
she will see the bare hedges
beyond the fallow fields —
only the perfumed jelly
recalls berry-picking time.

<19>

I Have Been to Ballylee

I have been to Ballylee
Climbed the steep stairs
to Yeats' old study
where the window
opens out to a view of the river
winding through the fields

<20>

On Seeing Maud Gonne, Dublin 1942

On the pavements, narrow Georgian houses
cast long summer shadows.
In the chestnut trees behind Trinity railings
a blackbird sang,
on an afternoon in war-time,
long ago.

In the green glass
of Johnston's window
I saw your reflection,
like a black swan on a lake,
moving slowly through the Dublin crowd,
a legend in mourning.

In age your beauty dimmed,
your melancholy gaze turned inward.
Were you remembering old dreams
or lamenting Yeats' Ireland?

You walked away towards Grafton Street.
Above you, gray gulls
keening in the pale sunlight,
sailed over the roof-tops
to Stephen's Green.

<21>

Neutral Territory

There were few cars then —
Only priests and doctors
Traveled the roads,
Both being considered
Absolute necessities.
Sometimes donkeys,
Hauling small loads,
Trotted through the Dublin streets,
Giving the city a rustic air.
The mailboat sailed from Dún Laoghaire
Carrying country boys and girls to work in England,
Or to join the "Forces" — no work at home for them.
Nights, especially during winter nineteen-forty,
The high drone of planes could be heard,
Crossing our pathetic air-space —
The Luftwaffe, on their way to shatter
Another English city.
We lay in our beds
And felt safe
In our proclaimed neutrality.
Something gallant in that act of defiance —
Because our neighbor was armed to the teeth —
And desperate.
One night I stood on a hill above the sea,
Green flashes lit up the horizon —
An air-raid was in progress
On the English court.
I felt a strange thrill —
A mixture of pity and the gut feeling — relief.
And something else — a shameful
"Thank God, not us, this time, but them."

<22>

Antinomian Age

But times have changed
the age of *anarchy* is here
Trust is destroyed and stiles abandoned
unspoken agreement compact
mindless disorder
chaos suspicion
Now the Antinomian Age
is here

<23>

Emergency

The distant sound of
boom in the night away
in the direction of Dublin.

The low droning sounds of
the German planes
going to bomb England.

The Kish light.[8]

The evening in Spring
when the mail boat
raced toward the
harbor. Sandycove bombed.

The night the Germans
bombed Dublin.

The night they
blitzed Belfast.

The feeling of isolation
the evening I watched
the green flares over the
water as a raid took place
on England.

---

[8] *Kish light*. A lightship moored above the Kish sandbank, located eight miles
East of Dún Laoghaire. Replaced in 1965 by a lighthouse.

<24>

Icarus 1944

Shuddering,
Climbing
Into a hot blue sky
Twisting,
Turning,
Silver as a little star.

Tearing,
Searing,
Lavender burst of flame
Star fire shining
Tumbling,
Falling,
Into the evening tide —
And no one saw.

<25>

The Hero[9]

Boots lined up in the Hero's kitchen.
He won't return to fill them now
And trudge over the Wicklow hills
Somber in their autumn colors.
He has gone where another wills.

The logs he cut are stacked by the driveway.
They will not warm him in winter now.
Reading by his cheerful fireplace
his dog stretched out
The Hero has finished with life's long race.

He lived his life at the edge of sadness
But cheerfully tried to do his best.
God grant there will be another meeting
In the place of peace he always sought
When I'll see his smile and hear his greeting.

Seek in room after room
Wander through his rooms
Everywhere orderly as though he knew.

---

[9] This poem describes the house of the poet's brother, Jim, as it was found upon his death in 1988.

<26>

Latest Fad

"What's the latest fad?"
snorted her brother.
"Before it was the IRA"
and indeed, her mother
thought with dismay
of her daughters

marching through the house
in heavy shoes, how
one daughter had assumed
a clipped, military way of
speaking.

Her mother had debated the
matter with the nuns.
Schoolwork was done,
they assured her, but
there had been an emphasis
on 1916 and the war of
independence.

In fact, one nun, who had been
her history teacher, said
"She holds forth by the
hour on that period and
England's treatment of Ireland
to the detriment of
everything else."

<27>

I Do Miss the Sea

in winter
white capped waves
racing in the bay
cascading over
the East pier
the water the color
of polished steel
a cutting
wind blowing
from the Bay East
making those of us
on our way home
think of warm fires
and cups of hot tea.

<28>

Table Manners (Early Version)

Those evenings, long ago
in winter
when we sat over tea
the shades were drawn
against the cold.
The fire sparked and sputtered
in the grate.
We were together
listening to old stories
of our parents' youth.
Our dog before the fire
reflection in mirrors
old paintings on wall
light over table
and a snowy white cloth
outside winter setting in.

We were all there —
a girl and her mothers
at home in Ireland
waiting out the war years.

We spoke of the day's news
the Russians holding out at
Stalingrad.
We listened to the BBC
a correct British voice.

<29>

Ancestors

There was a way to build a fire
forgotten now.
Twists of newspaper
in the cradle of the iron gate,
kindling laid cross-ways,
small pieces of coal
placed as on a cairn.
A match struck and threads of smoke
curled upwards.

We sat in a half circle,
worshippers at a shrine.
Watched headlines melt away
as the paper burst into flame,
fluttering rose and gold.
Fire forged a bond between us;
we spoke in low voices,
expressed loving thoughts,
retold old tales.

As the fire died,
coal crumbled to ash.
A small flame, electric blue
flickered in the hearth.
We heard a tiny sound,
a pleading voice,
protesting the act of extinction.

In the West of Ireland
people carried live coals
from an old hearth to a new house,
legend says, to forge a link
with ancestors.

<30>

My only link is memory.
There, the little fugue of flame
pleads and whispers,
accompanies the ghostly voices
echoing in my mind.

This poem is an earlier draft of the poem retitled
"Burning Coal."

<31>

Burning Coal

There was a way to build a fire,
forgotten now.
Twists of newspaper
in the cradle of the iron grate,
kindling laid crosswise,
small pieces of coal
placed as on a cairn.
We struck a match
and smoke curled upwards.

Irish winters, long ago,
we sat by the hearth,
watched paper burst into flame,
fluttering rose and gold,
and heard the crackle of
wood and coal.
It was cozy by the fire.
We chatted and told
old stories.

As the fire died a small flame
flickered in the hearth.
The coal crumbled to ash,
a chill entered the room.
Outside wind blew from
the wild Atlantic.
With good-night kisses
we went to bed
in our chilly rooms.

<32>

In the West of Ireland, long ago,
legend says, people carried live coals
from an old house to a new hearth —
a way to forge a link with ancestors.
My only link is memory.
In memory the little fugue of flame
jumps and whispers,
companion to the ghostly voices
whispering in my mind.

<33>

Abandoned Ceremonies

The ceremony of
carrying coals is gone —
laid to rest —
who carries coals these
days
days of the grinning
silent electric fire
heat with the life
gone out of it —
how impractical
uprooted
little ceremonies
abandoned.

Our animated voices filled
the shadowy room —
the little fugue of
flames an accompaniment
to our young laughter.

To recapture our long
gone conversations —

gone, like the rising
smoke
etherized in air.

<34>

The Last Tram, November 1949

Lamps extinguished, hours late,
the old train rumbles through Merrion Square,
last journey outward bound
to the Dalkey sheds.

Close as bees in a hive
tossing down the black brew,
youthful travelers roar out a dirge
on all things passing.

Bulbs wrenched from their sockets,
confetti-colored tickets grabbed,
old upholstery, thick as carpets,
cut into flitters.

Pressed by the driver's foot
the bell's persistent clanging
signals to rose-red houses —
the end of an era has arrived.

The citizenry, cold in the fog,
cheer the anachronism
lumbering down Mount Street,
rear light vanishing, a fading star.

<35>

Savoirse

Castle mains place
ruin
flag waving
child
Anglo-Irish
the English too
will have their day

<36>

Nineteen Fifty-Seven

Nineteen fifty-seven
I remember
reading
the Welsh poet's
sonorous verses
on my own
narrow, confining
island —

<37>

Patrick Kavanagh on Pembroke Road[10]

April on Pembroke Road.
Sudden showers soak the long gardens.
In the lilacs a blackbird sings,
daffodils light dark corners,
the sky is filled with promise.

Midday, the poet, solitary man,
plods up the street
on the way to McDaids[11]
to dispense homespun wisdom
to the usual blustering crowd.

His countryman's shoes
strike echoes from the pavement.
Arms folded on his chest,
old felt hat battened on his head,
lost in thought, he walks alone.

An outsider in urban exile,
far from the lanes of Inniskeen,
lonely as an old crow,
his days are lived
on the edge of poverty.

Hungry for female company
he greets the indifferent typist
on her way to lunch
at the Lansdowne Hotel.
She spurns his greeting.

---

[10] Patrick Kavanagh (1904-1967), poet and novelist, author of *The Great Hunger*.
[11] McDaids Pub is a haunt of poets and writers, located in Dublin.

<38>

No matter.
He trudges on to his Parnassus,
the banks of the Grand Canal
where the apologetic swan
awaits its exaltation.

<39>

Mass Day in the Church at Dalkey

I came through the door
nearest the altar.
The church smelled of candles
and stale incense.
At that door you paid sixpence.
Years later, I sat
in the organ loft —
that way I could sneak in
without paying anything.
I couldn't see paying sixpence
to hear the word of God.
Surely, either it was worth
more than sixpence
or it was beyond price
no Yeats' greasy coin
could satisfy.
From the top of the hill
we could hear the bell
beseeching us to hurry down
to Mass.
On clear winter mornings
over the skirling wind
it seemed to clamor for our
attention —
God in the church
beseeching us.

<40>

Poem on Visiting Bowers Court

Hot summer day
Dead crows metaphor
Ballyhoura Hills
words all down
silence
space where house
stood
small chapel
graveyard

<41>

Summer Evening at New Street

The garden wanders uphill to the trees,
A summer's growth, rain heavy,
Conceals the toad's lair;
And in the apple trees above,
The dappled fruit hangs succulent and fair.
Nearby a shadowed fountain leaps and falls;
In graceful cadence; Butterflies
With chalk-pale angled wings,
Scan the blossoming flower beds;
And in the verdant hedge a robin sings.
Shadows lengthen as the evening comes,
The wind sighs softly in the trees;
Through the woods, in slowly fading light;
The timid deer step daintily,
To gain some sustenance before the night.
One summer evening when the air was cool
We passed the time with friends
In this secluded place.
It gave our hearts tranquility and ease,
A benefit of blessings and of grace.

<42>

Achill

Where can I go for that great silence
on Achill long ago?[12]
I walked the roads at night
under a darkening sky
filled with stars
a full moon cresting in the east.
The air smelled of peat smoke.
The only sound
the hush and swell
of the Atlantic
and the distant barking of a dog
on a little mountain farm.

When I think of that silence,
those winding roads
white in the moonlight,
waves breaking under Minaun,
the seals sleeping by Clew Bay,
down the years I hear
like a blessing
the soft voices of the men of Keel
walking from the fields
bidding me a quiet
"Good-night."

---

[12] *Achill.* Describes the poet's 1958 stay with novelist Heinrich Böll and family in Keel, Achill Island.

<43>

To Sheelagh Kirby

In memory of the author of
The Yeats Country

I remember you, Sheelagh Kirby — long ago,
Sheelagh Flanagan then, grey-eyed,
warm, russet-haired schoolgirl
part of that gray convent landscape
cold as a rainy April Irish day.

Years passed, I wandered,
Lost and found the past.
In Sligo, dreamed dreams,
watched from the high rain-streaked window,
the clouds drift in gentle greyness over Riochree.

You came to seek me out at noon
an hour before departure time.
I hurried, late, through slate-grey Sligo leaves
too late I came, you'd gone forever.
When I came again to Sligo
you were memory,
still Sheelagh Flanagan, grey-eyed
in the convent shade.

<44>

Roan Inish

I saw a movie
about an island,
magical home to gulls
and gentle seals.

This was the story —
a child floated away
in a reed coracle,
was succored by seals,
protected by gulls.

In the pure Irish air
the gulls swooped
and glided above
the sun-warmed rocks
by the shore.
The barking seals
splashed in the waves.

Time passed,
the sea-child was found.
Restored to the nest
of its ancestors,
a stone cottage on the cliffs
of Roan Inish where,
there by the welcoming stove,
it remembered scenes
undreamed of
by its rescuers.

<45>

Nanny

What were they like
those girls
from the Irish countryside
who looked after us?

Ms McKeown
Ms Moran from Offally Lavis
Ms Byrne from Roscommon

I recall
their country accents
their infinite kindness
their simple faith

1920s coats fur collars
cloth hats
and their nanny
wheeling baby Dermot
in his pram with the
high wheels

Nanny, who laid down
the law
as we heard said

I remember those afternoon walks
along the unpaved country
roads winding
away from the surging
Shannon
surging through Westmeath

<46>

We walked obediently
one on each side of
my brother's Stanley stroller
(called by us a "go car")
Nanny following
baby Dermot sleeping
the afternoon away.

Simple daily pleasures
in the summer through
the daisied fields.
In autumn declining sun
winter's nipping frost
then spring and the
robins singing.

One day, thirty years ago
a knock on my door.
A smiling face framed
by white hair
an urgent request —
naming my old name.

Miss Byrne, here in America
an emigrant like myself
saying my old name
with, like me, an American
name, in an American accent.

But somewhere in those
vowels and syllables
I heard the soft sound of
the Irish country girl's voice

and in a rush of feeling
broke into tears.

<47>

Letter from Ireland

My friend wrote —
"We were on the Green Walk
above White Rock
when we saw a porpoise
leap and dive
in the sunlit sea
of early morning."

In a rush of memory
I recalled how, years ago,
from the same green place,
I watched this magical
leaping and plunging,
these agile creatures
swiftly disappearing
around the rocky coast
of the island.

<48>

Green Walk Above White Rock

In this decade
of poisoned waters
I had thought them
gone forever —
I mourned their passing.

This summer
when I am there
I will go to the Green Walk
above the White Rock
and watch for them
to suddenly appear
in the blue, sky reflecting sea.

In the heartstopping
leaps and dips
rise and fall
of their glistening bodies
in the gentle susurration
I will gain comfort —
something in spite of all
the terrible violations
endures to tell us give us
a beauty this heart-wrenching
beauty.

<49>

At Shannon Park

What one loves in
childhood stays
in the heart forever.
— Mary Jo Putney

There's a new way in to the old house.
The winding avenue is gone.
The trees cut down, the house looks stark,
no shadows on its gray walls,
its windows reflect the autumn sky.

Boys run and shout.
A ball hits tarmac down on the court
where we played tennis long ago.
A few elms, last of the woods
shelter the crows, descendants of those
that cawed in my childhood
and croaked down the chimneys
of my old home.

I am a ghost wandering here
where no one knows me.
A bell rings, boys drift to their
classrooms.
They are the future. I search for links
to a lost past.

Then I find, hidden in the undergrowth,
the stone urns my father filled
with flowers.

"At Shannon Park" is an earlier draft of
the poem retitled "Going Back."

<50>

Going Back

There's a new way in, now,
to the old house,
the winding avenue is gone.
Stripped of its shadowing trees,
painted a blinding white,
the house looks stark —
windows reflect the autumn sky.

Down on the court
the boys run and shout
as a ball hits the tarmac
where once there was grass,
green as emeralds, long ago.
A few old elms, last of the woods
shelter the ragged, noisy crows,
descendents of those
that cawed in my childhood.

Going back raises old ghosts,
more real than the crows.
I know the past is dead —
change, which is the future,
has obliterated it.
But I can't let it go.

A bell rings commandingly,
draws me back from remembering.
The boys run back to the classrooms,
they are not concerned with ghosts,
they connect to the future.
I seek a link to the past.
Then I found, hidden in the
undergrowth,
the stone urns my father
filled with flowers.

<51>

The Park

An old house acquires power over the heart with the course of time; it touches the imagination with a sense of life inherent in itself.

Coming here gives perspective and
direction.
This is where my life began
in Nineteen Twenty-One.
It was another country then
the pigeons cooed in the woods
the crows flocked
the old tower
in the fading evening light.
It was so silent
you could hear the leaves
rustling on the trees
in a west wind.
The house nestled
in the woods
like a secret
not easily found
without the most precise directions.

<52>

The Seat at Saval Park

Weathered now
close by the granite
wall
a public seat safely
outside the walled-in
garden —
no real contact
here —
the seat is for temporary
respite

<53>

Bisque

"Bisque," she said — it was
alone on an old table
in a Eunkerry shop —
"I'll let you have it cheap,"
she said, handing it to me:
the small figure of a
young girl, Victorian.
I looked at the small
white face,
saw myself if I had
died at thirteen, say.
Innocent —
outside the children
played conkers
in the October sunlight
shouting.
"It was an old lady's," she said.
"Last thing she ever sold."
I wondered
did she watch the light
passing over their features,
see herself those long
years ago?

<54>

Prayer

On a Spring day, sixty years ago
I walked into the woods
to the granite cliffs
above the Irish Sea.
All was silent.

Far from my island home
war raged on, barbarous,
devastating in its cruelties.
A world at peace
seemed far away.

Weighed by the thought
of endless suffering
I walked through the aisles of trees,
looking towards the distant hills
wreathed in cloud shadows.

Across the valley
a breath of wind came
and touched my face
like the caress of a loving hand.
I heard the faint rustle of Spring leaves.

I thought of Elijah when,
seeking a sign from Heaven,
he felt the earth shake, the wind, the thunder —
then the soft whisper of a voice
and knew he had been touched by the Lord.

Raising my arms I prayed
for the suffering world,
that peace would come.
The wind ceased and silence fell.
I went on my way comforted.

<55>

Friend (At the Bay)

> *Farewell, swift light!*
> *Our summers are too short.*
> —Baudelaire

I come to seek an
old identity,
where the sea sighs
eternal whispering,
where gulls wheel and wail
in a sad blue sky
like fading flowers
along the Green Walk.

Seduced by nostalgia,
returning again and again
to where we used to walk,
I am survivor and mourner
standing above the cliffs
which fall in granite folds
to the Irish Sea.

These breaking waves —
a slow, insistent susurration,
a metaphor underscoring time.
Here we walked quoting Baudelaire
who wrote of the poet's special calling,
of his suffering which gives
the creative urge
a sharper edge.

Mentor, teacher, friend,
remembering you
who set me on a path of creativity,
I write poems,
simple verses saying
like the sigh of the sea
there is a continuum.

<56>

In the Bay
a foghorn begins to moan,
mist curdles among the trees,
the birds are silent.
Walking away through the woods
I carry with me
a sense of your presence
of all that has passed
       into the air
             into the rain
                   into eternity.

*The next six poems are earlier versions
and variations of what became finalized
and titled "Friend (At the Bay)."*

<57>

Lost Loves

These hills are hardly changed
In forty years.
This was my world once —
The ghosts I think about today
Had lived here then.

Now I love them passionately,
And on these hills
I remember how it was,
In my young days.

The pines are full grown now
But the same pathway
Winds among their cool shadows
A dim radiance
Pierced by sunlight.

The gulls, flying in from the sea,
Wheel and cry
In the cool air.
Below me I hear the waves
Breaking on the far sea-shore.
A slow, insistent susurration —
an aqueous clock, underscoring time.

I look out over the water,
I once knew its every mood —
And I think of the old man,
Who sat gazing out to sea,
Remembering his drowned son.
Wind rises from the sea,
Wisps of mist curdle among the trees —
The birds are silent.
Down in the bay, the foghorn,
Haunting, evocative,
Begins to moan.

<58>

An Old Place

Years since I walked these hills.
Gulls wheel in the autumn air
wailing,
below I hear waves
break on the stony shore
an aqueous clock
underscoring time.

The past lies heavy
there's too much of long ago.
Trying to recapture it
is futile —
better just to savor
this old place.

I think of the old man
who everyday sat gazing
out to sea.
Time had stopped for him
when his son was lost
in the war.

Mist curdles among the trees,
the birds are silent.
I walk back to the village
down the unending path
into the present
pursued by the sigh
of the sea.

<59>

Remembering Killiney Bay

This was my world once
now most are gone
who knew me then.
I am a visitor
from a far country.

Alone in these hills
what happiness I feel —
it is as it used to be,
long years ago.

At the old stone wall
above the rocky quarries
blackberry and valerian bloom —
the scented yellow gorse
stabs the air.

Below me the waves
break on the rocky shore,
the flashing leap of porpoises
just as I remember.

Evening falls.
A soft mist rolls
in from the sea.
Soon the hills and valley
will be covered
with a pall of gray.
On the distant headland
the familiar light winks
a signal of caution,
guardian of the Bay.

<60>

Wisps of mist curdle among the trees.
The birds are silent.
The Kish light
sends its familiar signal.
Somewhere a fog horn
begins to moan.
Far below me
the familiar sound —
the Bray-to-Dublin trains.
How many times
I traveled that
familiar line
almost since childhood.

<61>

Killiney

Pale sunlight floods the hills,
Strikes sparks from the granite —
It is silent, only the gulls
Call and shimmer in a cloudless sky.
Hard to believe I once lived here.

To visit again the three hills
Beloved in childhood
Lying between Dalkey and Killiney
Above the Irish Sea
Is happiness.

I wander through the pines
A dim radiance of cool shadows
Pierced by sunlight
The earth a carpet of pine needles
Each footstep releasing their spicy scent
On the autumn air.

At the old stone wall
Above the rock quarries,
Blackberry and valerian bloom
And the scented yellow gorse
Stabs the air.

Below me I hear the waves
Breaking on the far sea shore.
A slow, irrevocable susurration
And a cool wind rises from the sea,
Where I once saw the flashing
Leap of porpoises and
Remembered the old man
Whose son was lost at sea
Sitting, gazing out over the
Rippling water.

<62>

The wisps of mist
Curdle among the trees.
The birds are silent.
Down in the bay the foghorn
A dirge for all that's lost
Haunting, evocative
Begins to moan.

<63>

At Killiney Bay

Summer is gone from these shores
there is sadness in the air.
Below me the sea sighs
an eternal whispering.
Is is for those who are no more
or my lost self, years ago?
Gulls wheel and wail in a sad blue sky
like fading flowers along the Green Walk.

The waves break with a slow susurration
on the stony shore of Killiney Bay.
Here I am survivor and mourner
inexorably drawn to a receding past.
Seduced by nostalgia I return again and again
to stand alone above the cliffs
steeply falling into granite folds
down to the sighing Irish Sea.

<64>

Continuum

The voices of the gulls
are the same,
the hills unchanged.
I know each tree and every
nook and cranny.
I walked here discussing
Baudelaire with you
who wrote of the
poet's suffering
his special calling
and how suffering purifies
and ultimately gives
to the creative urge
a sharper edge.
Now I write poems
simple verses, saying
ultimately, life is good,
suffering has meaning.
Like the unceasing sigh of the sea,
there is a continuum.

<65>

Three Rock Mountain

Dublin, Ireland

Your gentle slopes a backdrop
to the spires and towers
of my old city,
crowned by your massive boulders,
three sentinels watching over the valley.

Walking up there in sunlight
I could see down the distant
Georgian streets and squares
and beyond, the blue stretch
of Dublin Bay.

When I think of you I am uplifted.
Your bogs and uplands,
a palette of soft browns and greens;
your gentle slopes bathed
in the golden light of a summer morning.

The best time was evening,
perhaps in autumn,
when the city twinkled
and the lighthouses sent beams
out across the water.

Then, as I hiked,
I'd hear the birds below me,
a last evening chorus
singing your praises,
dear mountain of soft shoulders.

<66>

On Hearing the Baily Will Lose
Its Light Keeper

Christmas 1995

Sweeping over the dark
winter waters
I watched the Baily
sentinel on the peninsula
send its shining beams
across Dublin's stormy bay.

All my early days
it was a comfort
on winter nights
and I thought of the keeper
in his little house
adjacent to the simple light.
This was his sacred trust —
to warn the ships of hidden
shoals and
mark the coast of Dublin's bay.
Today I hear the keeper
will have the light click on
and off in solitude —
automation has arrived
and the sacred trust
is transferred
to a nameless machine
for the first time
since 1665.

<67>

The Secret at the Heart of the Rose

a steady flame, the
gold glow of a sanctuary lamp,
the silence before the
empty tomb
the person met with or the
empty road
the words of comfort and
the upraised hand

<68>

Dún Laoghaire

That last day in Ireland,
early one morning
in an Irish summer,
I watch the cormorants
on the rocks that line the shore
of Dublin Bay.
Wings outstretched
they face seawards
sway gently
from side to side.
The water, to the far horizon
reflects the autumn sky.

These birds move
stretch and bend
in harmony with the lapping waves.
As the sun rises higher
they turn to its thin warmth —
then, one by one they dive
into the long fingers of sunlight
stroking the sea.

At low tide tomorrow
they will repeat this ritual
but I will be far
from this familiar place.
The great bay, the gentle hills
the cry of the sea birds
and, at night, far off
the winking lights
of the old lighthouses
ever vigilant,
ever there.

<69>

Irish Summer

Early one morning
I watched the cormorants
wings outstretched
on the rocks
on the shore
of Dublin Bay.

They faced seawards,
moving gently
from side to side,
the water
to the far horizon
a chilly, distant blue.

The birds rocked slowly
as if to music
in avian Tai Chi,
stretching and bending
in harmony with
the waves.

As the sun rose higher
they turned to its thin warmth,
greeting the morning.
Then, one by one, they dived
into the long fingers of sunlight
stroking the whispering sea.

<70>

A Backward Look

Remembering the joyous chorus of birds
in early morning and
in the last rosy glow of tranquil evenings
the crows returned to the elms
and the sea gulls returned
to the sea.

<71>

Stone from Rifearta

The stone
from Rifearta
is on my window sill —
I cup it in my hands
cold as ice
this little stone
from where once
the humble poor
knelt by the graves
of the Kings of Leinster.

<72>

Sea Change

The country that I dream about
is gone.
Gone with the corncrake
from the old meadow
behind our house.
It used to call on
summer evenings when the pale moon
rose huge over Dalkey Hill.
Now the quiet ways are gone,
the old romance is dead.

And they also are gone
who led quiet lives.
Now the busy world intrudes,
the landscape altered,
the green spaces gone.

Where is the life
on those hills above
the Irish Sea?
It is altered, altered
eternally.

<73>

Endless Change

I came too late to the hills, they were
swept bare
of all that prompted memory.
Going there, filled with desire
to recreate a long gone past
has left me bereft of hope
that somehow, the past survives
life's endless changing.

<74>

Ireland Unseen

There are places in Ireland
that I've never seen. I'll never see.
I ask myself — how it is possible
I've never seen the Nier Valley
or Dunquin?
My mother once said "go to
Donegal — it's haunting."
I never did. I chose to leave.
I yearned to get away.
Spent those wartime years
dreaming of Spain, Italy, the USA.
Now in age I yearn
to sit by the sea
at Ballyvaughan,
to return even to Wicklow
watch the dawn
break above
the Irish Sea
drive down the Sally Gap in spring
hear the lambs cry and watch
and the sparrow hawk
on the wing, swooping
earthwards, silent killer from an empty sky.
I want to visit Céide fields
go to the Beara —
I am filled with longing.

<75>

Alternate Lifestyle

What if I'd never left Ireland?
I'd be sitting alone, in the old house
waiting for your letters
postmarked where?
America, Australia, Europe

and I'd weep for your presence
think of how I feel each time
the phone rings
it might be one of you.

Nothing worse than exile, I think
for those who go
a little less than those
who stay behind.

Waiting, always waiting
for the sound of the mailman's step
or the persistent ring of the phone
living on hope and memory
trying to show the brave
side of things.

<76>

Europe In and After WWII

9 Sept 1939

Over my world shadows chase
shadows the distant towns
shiver — anticipation of terror
breathholding among citizens
no sun shines — harsh voices
threaten — sea below
looks calm the mountains close
no sound — only the birds
the waiting thousands hurry
to do what has to be done.

<79>

Wir hatten uns gefürchtet . . .

We were afraid . . .

I can hardly remember
what my Austrian friend
told me
that autumn day
long ago
in the sad city
of Graz.

I asked him
"When the Jews were banned
from the towns
and the synagogues
stood silent and empty
did you feel pity
or maybe shame?"

I think he told me,
"No, it did not
concern us,
we wanted only
to survive.
*Wir hatten uns
gefürchtet.*"

I thought
of those others
on the trains going east
believing, somehow,
it was also only
a matter
of surviving.

And the tall chimney
beckoned
on the horizon.

<80>

Teddy Bear Coat

Where did my Teddy
Bear coat go?
Bought in Selfridges in
1958
London — how easy then
to walk the streets at
night
and the police man
directed me to
an Underground —
and life was kinder
simpler
we wore our hair in
smoother curls
our heels were higher
and white gloves were
de rigeur —
she looks out of her picture
eminently pleased with
the world.
Were we really wearing
such hats in 1961?
I saw a picture of
Valerie E.
standing with the poet
en route to America —
on her head what
looked like the wings of a
bird perched
as if ready to fly
off into the English Spring.

<81>

She was wearing a Teddy
Bear coat —
who knows of Teddy
Bear coats now?
Now they have, for me
all the tender poignancy
of an artifact from afar.

<82>

Buckingham Palace

The Queen came out of Buckingham Palace
The sun shone light all over the land
She was wearing a robe of rose-red chablis
and she carried a parasol in her hand

The crowds just loved the *great* occasion
They saw the twinkling of her crown
They hardly needed any persuasion
Their cheers went ringing through town

Out on the balcony came the princes
Accompanied by their sprightly wives
They all wore hats with grosgrain ribbon
They were having the time of their lives

The little prince, his blond hair shining
Waved to the crowd below
From the large brass band to the traffic
They put on quite a show

Oh what a day it was in London
The relics of a time long past
I wondered as I stood by the fountain
Just how long this farce would last.

<83>

The Day I Sang to Cows

Cornwall, England

Above the cliffs in Cornwall
meadows are home to cows —
They look out over gated fences
with a gentle benign gaze.

One summer day long ago
I watched their slow movements
listened to the soft crunch of their jaws
as they chewed meadow hay.
Watching their gentle presence
I sang an old Irish song.

The grazing animals, heads raised
gazed in my direction.
They were as attentive as children
to a lullaby.

One by one they slowly walked
to the barred gate.
A few uttered soft *moos*
thrusting their heads forward
to see the singer.

When I ceased to sing they stayed
crowding at the gate,
their mellow gaze fixed on me,
a stranger who sings to cows.

<84>

The Lions of Rome

In the hot summer season
when the air is still,
in the soft darkness,
beyond the gardens of the Villa Borghese,
a sound is heard —
it is the night-time calling
of the lions in the Roman Zoo.

On these hot nights,
the imprisoned lions
are a constant reproach.
They articulate their loss,
full of longing
for the savannah
and the nocturnal hunt.

We pen them up, the wild things.
We savor a cheap thrill,
watching those massive jaws,
while we, safe beyond the bars
observe their golden eyes
looking into the endless distances,
beyond the Sunday crowds.

<85>

The City Astonishing[1]

Lightly pearled on the
water
giant
sandstone
eagles
over entrance
peeling paint
eerie objects
crutches
trunks
Hamburg America line
silent voices

---

[1] Based on a visit to New York's Ellis Island, but linked chronologically to the poems in this section..

<86>

Eurasian
Influence

Soldier's Tale 1955

Come with me the soldier said
his eyes sad and lonely —
it is long ago now
but I have to tell you
how I felt when we marched
through the fields of sunflowers
in the Ukraine.

We were interlopers
striding through the fields
past ranks of golden faces
of the sunflowers
their innocence unaware
of our deathly mission.

Sometimes I feel like going
back to Ukraine —
to stand by the fields
and tell those golden beauties
how bitterly regret lies
on my Teutonic soul.

<89>

Xristos Voskres[1]

The protestant church
The silence
The ikon
Myself Irish Catholic
thinking of old Russia
known only from the classics —
Tolstoy, Dostoyevsky, Chekhov

---

[1] *Xristos Voskres*. Russian. Christ is Risen.

<90>

Hymn for America

God bless this dear Country
and let its righteous men prevail.
Let the sons of Jefferson
and the daughters of Mother Jones
come out and praise the Lord
on the commons and Main Streets
of the little towns.
Let them sing *Hallelujah*
for all the good that exists
between the coasts
the flat lands and
the mountains.
Let them swing back to
goodness and caring
and when the redwings sing
let our hearts answer
Hallelujah.

<91>

Laika

Laika,[2] the spacecraft
crossing the sky at
night, and as it
passed dogs suddenly
began to bark.

---

[2] *Laika* was the dog, a part-Samoyed terrier, on the Russian spacecraft *Sputnik 2*, launched on November 3, 1957. The anecdote related here took place when Moira was in the back garden of her mother's house in Dún Laoghaire.

<92>

Indo-China (June 26, 1972)

Is it the end or the beginning?
That October they smashed the windows
And the lamps in the auditorium were shattered,
They raged and rampaged against the truth,
The bitter truth of Indo-China.

It was October then but I still remember
The fat boy with red hair and a camera
Who jeered the man who was told the truth,
The bitter truth of Indo-China.

That was seven years ago and now
Enraged, youth spews forth its anger
Flowers, not guns, they scream —
We know the bitter truth of Indo-China.

Last night a call from the nation's capital
Alerted me to unsuspected dangers,
My loved one witness to the truth,
The bitter truth of Indo-China.

<93>

Vietnam Christmas '67

The children lie in their hospital beds,
Great white bandages wreath their heads.
Christmas shining in their eyes,
Ready for the great surprise.

Smart young nurses sit around,
Tap their white shoes on the ground,
Sing in voices sweet and clear:
Peace to all throughout the year.

Out of door the wild guns boom.
Rockets blast and aircraft zoom.
But within the lamplit room
Merry thoughts dispel the gloom.

Smiling soldier at the door
Enters now with jolly roar
"Ho-ho-ho, dear girls and boys,
Here I come with Christmas toys."

Red and white his wooly gown
And his great white beard flows down.
All the children smile and cheer,
"Yankee Father Christmas here."

In Santa's arms a great fat sack
And from another on his back
Peek forth all the Christmas toys
Sent by American girls and boys.

Loud and clear the voices ring
"Merry Christmas" — let us sing
And from each small snowy bed
Peeks a round, black Asian head.

<94>

Down the ward dear Santa walks
Giving here a doll that talks
Laying there a dog that barks
And a box of colored chalks.

Now the toys are almost gone
At the bed of Lan Thuy Lon.
Lan Thuy is very hard to see
wrapped in bandages from neck to knee.
Outside on a sunny day
All the people ran away
As the gleaming bird of steel
Dropped flames on the paddy field.

Ruined there, the blackened toys
Joys of village girls and boys
But, inside this cozy room,
Merry thoughts dispel the gloom.

<95>

Vietnam Christmas 1969

The children lie in their clean white beds.
There are many bandaged heads.
Attached to tortured arms and legs,
weights hang from the ceiling pegs.

Starched young nurses sit around,
Tap their white shoes on the ground,
Sing in voices sweet and clear,
"Peace to all throughout the year."

The children's eyes are shining bright.
Someone's told them that, this night
is a very special one,
full of *amitié*, and cheer, and fun.

Smiling soldier at the door
Enters now with jolly roar:
"HO HO HO, dear girls and boys,
Here I come with Christmas toys."

Red and jolly is his gown
And his great white beard flows down
And his great black combat boots
Shine so much it hurts to look.

In his arms a great fat sack
And another on his back
Stuffed quite full of Christmas toys
Sent by Yankee girls and boys.

Far away the wild guns boom.
Soldiers shoot and aircraft zoom.
The children are quiet in the lamplit room
Where merry thoughts dispel the gloom.

<96>

In China

In China
my friend said
every space grows
something edible
there are no lawns
only in parks
but there are flowers
because a flower
takes little room
just one flower
can make a difference
and you need
something to cheer you —
a flower
heartens you
like a smile
from a stranger
said my
Chinese friend.

<97>

Australia
Remembered

Outback

A Found Poem from a 2010 Conversation

Summer sun scorches spare scenery,
the great open spaces.
Dermot and I share the
tremendous vastness.

I pet a kangaroo,
only on the nose,
then he runs
into the sun.

<101>

Antarctic
Blast

Snowfall

Walking in the falling snow
another world takes hold,
one becomes aware of silence.
Slowly, one begins to feel
the helplessness of man in Nature.
All we can do, all we have achieved
is as nothing.

Before this relentless falling
laying a white blanket
that changes everything,
snow causes one to shiver
at its compacted coldness.
The only color the sky
a hard and brilliant blue
and an east wind
mocking man's efforts
to struggle through.

<105>

A Is for Africa

A is for Aardvark

My young son[1]
loved the name
Aardvark —
it captured his
imagination
and for days
he spoke
of that animal
in far-away
Africa —
even asked if
we could have
a pet
Aardvark —
then he saw
a picture
of one
in a textbook —
it was not
the animal
of his
imagination —
it didn't look
like anything
much
so he decided
he didn't like
Aardvarks
after all.

---

[1] *Young son*. Stefan Bailis.

<109>

Practice Run for Africa

The old garden is falling asleep,
the last summer roses droop
in a heavy mist.

Swallows swoop,
form into battalions,
line up on the wires.
Two small ones dive
over the chonta tree —
a practice run for Africa.

Only the robins will stay
claim their place again.

The sun is low in the sky.
Hedges throw long shadows
across the fields.
The cattle move slowly
look for a blade of grass.
In the wood a huge beech
a golden blaze against the sky.
Last summer roses droop
in a heavy mist.
The old garden is falling asleep.

<110>

South of
Our Border

Sol

Your bronze faces
glares, pitiless.
An avenger
out to get me.

There's no hiding
from you.
I avert my eyes
from your cruel
visage.

In the parched trees
the birds sit,
beaks open
in silent horror.

<113>

Pearls in Pink Cups

Hushed silence
and a darkening sky.
In the west
a sad luminosity.
A rising wind
flurries the tree tops.

Taps on the window pane,
those first, hesitant drops.
Soon the air is filled
with sound,
the falling rain.

Each drop an imprint
on the dark earth.
Rain on the needles
of hemlocks,
sparkles of light.
Rain in the bright
impatiens,
pearls in pink cups.
Over all a mistiness.

A steady syncopation
in the rain's drumbeat,
a feeling of renewal,
the smell of wet grass.
A ray of sun
pierces the clouds,
a brilliant bow arches
over the tree tops.

In the Atacama in northern Chile,
it rains once in fifty years.
If children have never seen rain,
how can they imagine it?

<114>

Summer Storm

The sky darkens
flashes
of dazzling light
crash from above —
world-ending
reverberations,
a minute's silence
and the show
repeats itself.

I stay back
from windows
fearful of
fusillades
and
fierce clamor.

The gentle patter
of raindrops
steadily quickens.

In the distance
one last flash —
heavy rain
pours down.

<115>

Tocsin at Waslala, Nicaragua

Mars burns, a red eye,
Over the innocent landscape.
All is silent on the coffee farms.
A warm wind rises,
Insidiously,
The flame burns low —
The air is full of sighs.

Above the mountains,
A ringed moon soars —
In the budding wood
Shadows lengthen.
An owl hoots,
Mournfully,
The sound ices the blood.

Over the border,
Assassins plot
Their maps of death,
Nailing the innocent to night —
A distant tocsin sounds —
Glamorously.

Light shatters the horizon.
Above the coffee farms
A sullen sound of thunder.
Echoes from the mountains —
The cowards penetrate the villages
And terrorize the people —
I hear their distant cries.

<116>

Monarchs

Forty years ago, in late summer
I saw them flit across my garden
and alight on the fast-fading flowers.

I was told "They are on their way to Mexico
two thousand five hundred miles away."

I took out my map of North America
and traced their routes with my finger
marveling at their long migration.

Today I read with deep sadness
their sanctuary at Oyamel
is being ravaged.

Imagine I think to myself
perhaps 40 million butterflies
landing in American gardens
on their way south
only doing what they've always done
obeying a law of nature

that, unknown to them
enables us to hold our breath
when we see their scarlet bodies
and velvet wings
soar above our heads
on sunny, summer days.

<117>

Crossing Canada
And America

Reading the Weather

Nov 8, 1996

The weather report tells me
today at 30,000 feet over southwest Canada
a harbinger of flooding rains
is forecast for the Northeast.
The all-seeing weather balloons
transmitted the alarming news
that jet stream winds were blowing,
approaching 180 miles an hour
over southwest Canada.

It is predicted that these winds
will plunge into the base of
a trough of low pressure
over the Mississippi Valley
and will intensify.
They will rattle windows and
toss down trees.
At the same time, a river
of humid air
from the balmy Gulf of Mexico
will surge northward
ahead of a cold front
setting the stage for protracted rain.

Along the Middle Atlantic seaboard
potent thunderstorms are possible
and from the Great Lakes
to the Appalachians
the heaviest rain will fall.
Tonight parts of the Poconos and
the Catskills will receive
an autumnal blessing,
four to five inches of rain.
Tomorrow this beneficence
will press into New England.

<121>

Snow will accumulate on
Lakes Superior and Michigan
and tomorrow Lakes Erie
and Ontario
will be the recipients
of this wintry blast.

But in far California
temperatures will reach 90 degrees
and in the balmy waters
of the Pacific
bathers will hardly
be able to imagine
the slow and steady progress of
our eastern winter creeping like a stealthy thief
stealing away our warmth and color

the failing light
the slow fall of the leaves
and the weakened suncasts
illuminating a paler sky.

<122>

Sighting Land

coming in on plane
seeing contrails in
western sky

compare to seafarers
smell of pine trees
sight of more birds

<123>

Wood

These days I am consumed
by anger —
a conservationist by nature
and by choice
I fret and fume
reading of the mindless clearing
of the western forests
the demand for wood
by our burgeoning society.
A demand insatiable, unmindful
of our children's future,
when, unless we find another way
they will ask
when we speak of woodland
"Mommy — what is wood?"

<124>

South Rim

Oh canyon[1] I know
my head before you
your terraces
folding and folding
below the sharp
outline of the rim
against a translucent sky

I want to protect you
keep you as secret
as you were before
we came in our jeans
and denim caps

---

[1] From a 1999 visit to the Grand Canyon with Jack Bailis.

<125>

Coming from Fort Worth

It was about
twilight
he said

The old train[2]
came round the bend
speeding towards me
out of the past
the chuffing of the
1896 engine
the infinitely sad wail
of the whistle
the rattle of wheels
on the tracks

I think of the time this
old engine thundered
across the prairies
with its haunting call
and the wife
standing at the door of her sod house
devoured by loneliness
thought of home
watched the sun sink below
the western rim of the prairie
and broke into tears.

---

[2] A 1996 description and photos of the Tarantula train, which runs daily from
Forth Worth to Grapevine, provided by Stefan Bailis to his mother, evoked this
poem.

<126>

Crossing the Des Moines in Autumn

Air like wine
palest blue autumn sky
Trees barely changing
color
Distant hoot wail of a
train whistle
In the distances planes taking
off
freshness   buoyancy

Slow flowing river
sun striking sparks from
metal posts
orange red leaves
of a maple tossing
in the light breeze
Somewhere in the city
bell tolls, slowly —
a time to move on

<127>

Winterset

That day, in Winterset
the leaves were turning gold and red
the festival was in full swing
community spirit filled the streets.
The young girl in culottes and
a spangled dress
sang her heart out
her voice soared over the rooftops
of this old and lovely town
in the heart of America.
On the steps of the courthouse
a woman sang of lonely roads.
Something in this crowd
of an older America —
good humored togetherness
and a spirit of conviviality.

<128>

Winterset Revisited

Someday I'll go to Winterset again.
I'll stand where we stood
listening to a girl singing
of happiness.
That day there was a street fair
celebrating summer on the prairies
in their lovely town.

Children ran through
aisles between the booths.
Folks walked slowly around.
Somehow no one seemed hurried.
It all was as it should be
on a prairie summer day.

<129>

Thinking About Minneapolis

It's 2 pm now, in Bloomington.
The folks are playing tennis at
International Village
and the traffic moves
up to the city
down to the suburbs.
This is how I imagine it.

Under a high blue sky
the 15 lakes near Bloomington
shimmer
and folks are walking the trail
at Mendota
and in the Red Wing folks are
dining in the St. James Hotel
where the Pentecostalist waiter
serves with elegance and kind words.
On the tracks the 500 slowly goes
past Red Wing or the Mississippi.
Out at the locks on the river
visitors, tourists listen as a guide
describes the history.

Up on the hill at St. Paul
the dark basilica watches over
the comings and goings.
Everything is OK in Minneapolis,
the Minneapolis of my mind.

<130>

Heartland

An infinity of cornfields
stretch to the horizon —
the sky a blue translucence.
Nothing has prepared me
for this spacious land
indented with lakes,
held in a clarity of light.

Through the window
a shift in perspective:
the astonishing Cities —
glass-and-steel towers
yoked by the legendary river,
autumn colored.

A piercing beauty
in this minimalist landscape —
an economy of trees, houses, roads,
everywhere the shining waters —
something in this view
evokes a memory:
myself, an Irish child
reading Longfellow
and trying to imagine
Minnesota.

This poem was published under the alternate titles of "Coming Into the Heartland by Air" and "Coming Into the Heartland."

<131>

Mississippi Death Trip

In memory of Emmett Till,
murdered for whistling,
Mississippi, August 1955

Free and easy
in his youth,
how could he know
the dangers of that place,
the hostile stare,
blood-rush of hate?

He must have come
lighthearted
to the tenant farm
"visiting folks"
on the snow-white fields —
the Magnolia State.

A thousand
silenced voices
should have cried
"Son, take care."
A moment of silly fun,
a simple whistle
would seal his fate.

Beaten face.
Bullet in the head.
At the Tallahatchie River
his spirit fled.
Why didn't
sleeping birds
cry out in dread?

<132>

Justice comes
on slow, reluctant feet
for this doomed boy.
How long must he wait?
His ghost cannot
be laid to rest.
It is getting late.

<133>

The Museum at Cullowhee

In North Carolina
I saw a people's heritage
preserved in showcases:
a map, sea routes
of Scots-Irish migration,
a plough, a spinning wheel.
Symbols of men and women
who made the mountains home.

In the darkened room
of a thatched cottage
hauled stone by stone from Ireland,
a grate with its stack of peat,
wicker baskets, tin plates.
Artifacts in a candlelit tomb.
I looked at the small objects,
in their simplicity
beautiful as children's faces.

A woman beside me whispered,
"Do you know Ulster?"
Her voice an emigrant's longing.
A wind came up as we spoke,
rustling the autumn-colored forests.
The names blew away from us,
vanishing like the ghosts of settlers
in the blue mists
of the Smoky Mountains.

<134>

Heritage

In this museum at Cullowhee
I see a people's heritage:
an old map, sea routes
of Scots-Irish migration,
a rusty plough,
a spinning wheel —
symbols of men and women
who made these mountains home.

In the dimly-lit room
of a thatched cottage
hauled stone by stone
from Ulster:
simple plates, tin spoons,
a grate with its stack of peat —
artifacts in a candlelit tomb.

I look at the small objects,
in their simplicity
beautiful as children's faces.
A woman comes up to me;
Hearing me speak she asks,
Do you know Derry, Armagh, Portadown?
In her voice an exile's longing
a need to say the names.

A wind comes up as we speak
and the names blow away from us
across the valley,
vanish like the ghosts
of settlers in the blue mists
of the Smoky Mountains.

<135>

Spillway

The names
came spilling
out — Fermanagh, Connemara,
Sligo, Roscommon —
like an incantation
an urgency to
name them all
to me as if she
was offering a
prayer
incantation
that must be
offered to invoke
remembrance
an incantation
far from
Fermanagh
and I think of
Boa and the enigmatic heads[3]
too far to go often
spiritual country
and I think of
the Cherokees
over the mountains
our brothers in suffering
and the forced
migration of 1827
the pain of separation and
the longing
spelled out in
names

---

[3] Boa is an island near the north shore of Lough Erne, in County Fermanagh, Northern Island, home to the famous Iron Age stone figures depicted on the cover of this book.

<136>

Fontana

I'd say *Fontana, Fontana,*
Fontana
like a litany
as though
by repetition
I would physically evoke
the smoke-wreathed
mountains
and the cold blue lake
reflecting the autumn sky
nestled in
surrounded by forest
in western North Carolina.

<137>

Fiddle Music

I'm told that Indians
hated fiddle music.
It must have grated on
their nerves
unsettled them
these strange, thin,
drawn-out sounds,
sometimes like a weeping voice
crying.

On soft evenings in
the Appalachian Mountains
the Scots-Irish played dance tunes —
steps from the old country
assuaged their nostalgia.
I imagine the stamp and
beat of a hundred feet
on the wooden floors of shacks.

And in the mountains
sitting by their silent drums
the Indians listened
and were afraid
these eerie sounds
the piercing scrape and pitch
bow on string
filling the air
was not like anything
they knew —
the hoots and hollers
as the Scots-Irish
brought a culture
as old as the old tunes
resonant of the distant homeland
hearts uplifted
around them the
blue-hazed mountains.

<138>

Evocative times
homesickness momentarily
dispelled
violins sighing and sobbing
down the leafy coves
over the mountains in the
distant hollows.

<139>

Cherokee Poet

Her dark Cherokee eyes
serious —
"Listen," she said.
"Never use the words *dead*,
death or *died*.
We say 'Passed into Spirit.'"
I was consoled more
than I can say,
a few words spoken
by a Cherokee Poet,
from the mountains
in North Carolina.

<140>

Antietam

That day, walking down
the Sunken Road
hard to imagine
the huddled bodies
lying dead after the battle.
I remembered
Brady's photo.

It was a warm May day —
a little westerly breeze
rustled the corn stalks
in the field behind
a rough stone wall.

<141>

Grosse Île

Quebec, Canada

A summer rain dapples the St. Lawrence,
faint cries of riverbirds
break the silence,
the Laurentians,
brooding, gigantic,
loom on the northern shore.

Grosse Île lies
downstream from Quebec.
Its wooded shores fretted by water,
pines bend inland
by withering winter winds.
Its highest point crowned
by a Celtic cross.

I come to Grosse Île
pay homage to the Irish
sent across the Atlantic
in the coffin ships
their hopes flickering
like dying fires.

That summer of 1847[4]
ships sailed up the river,
sometimes forty in a line
to the small island,
grass pink with mallow,
loosestrife purple in the green.

---

[4] Many Irish immigrants fleeing the Famine died en route, and many others
were so weak and ill that they perished soon after arriving.

<142>

The wind sighs in the pine trees,
riverbirds cry distantly.
I wander along the leafy paths
think about the thousands
who died in this small place.
The only evidence that they lived,
five white crosses
in the silent valley.

<143>

Dreamers

"In their dreams there drifted canoes with great white wings like giant birds."
— 16th Century Micmac vision

As the ships weighed anchor
near the end of summer,
they had to believe
everything was possible.
There was no going back.

Somber woods a rampart
beyond the shore.
In the cove
the simple sand
without footprints.

In the hot evening
the women struck camp,
spoke softly.
They must have feared
the immense silence.

The men, black clad,
shouldered muskets.
Clouds of mosquitoes
hummed a terrifying chorus,
an enormous moon
rose over the ocean.

The voyagers' prayers
sonorous on the evening air
drifted from this small space
on the edge
of the continent.

<144>

Deep in the woods
the dreamers
who had foretold
"canoes with white wings
like giant birds
floating towards the shore"
watched the winking campfires.

Peering into the dark
they both could not
have imagined
what they had never seen,
other than in dreams.

<145>

Akewesasne

I said "An Irish name?"
The Indian woman looked
proud and determined.
"Akewesasne," she said
as though intoning a prayer.
"It means 'where the partridge drums'."
I apologized.
"I did not know," I said.
"Nobody knows," she responded.
"It is our old name
before all of you came."

That afternoon the Mohawks
asked me to dance.
I felt honored,
an outsider
invited into this community
on the banks of the St. Lawrence.

<146>

The Loss of the *Dorchester,* February 1943

On the phone from Minnesota
my son tells a story
about a friend.

In the dark days of
nineteen-forty three
an American ship set out
with over 900 young Americans
along the coast
of North America
to Greenland.

Off the coast of Greenland
the German submarine lurked
in dark and freezing waters.

I try to think of the
men, racing to their stations
when the torpedo struck
and the end of their world
had come in rushing water.

<147>

The Farm at Derry

Frost's New Hampshire farm
stands by a winding road.
Near it, Hyla Brook
echoes among the stones.

In the net of my
imagination
I pictured the farm
eighty years ago
with apple orchards
and a garden.

Now an empty field
girdled by walls of stone
stretches to the woods.
The field is bound
by markers.

Today, the house is closed.
Through the window
I see furniture of the period,
a few books on a table,
an old lamp.

Frost's farm is now
a place of reference
in the Mobil guide.
There is no trace of him
at Derry.

<148>

Yet I see
in a sheltered corner
a last few Bluets.
I pick them
remembering
"The Tuft of Flowers"

as blue as the poet's eyes.

<149>

At Frost's Grave

At the grave I look at the headstone
the familiar names —
Robert, Eleanor, Lesley —
and the daughter who died in childhood.
I think of the great voice
silenced now —
yet I am wrong.
Surely, as long as poets declaim your words
you live on, Robert Frost.

<150>

Wreath from Vermont

The cold light splinters
in a thousand fragments on the snow.
Sparrows flutter at the feeder.
The sun smiles in a pale-gold sky,
and a box arrives from Vermont.
I open it. Suddenly
the warm room is Vermont.
The imprisoned balsam,
released, perfumes the warm air.
The tight cones smell of forest.
I think of that far-off place
under deep snow,
the ice-trimmed shores of the lakes
hushed save for a wind from Canada
tinkling the branches of the trees.
In the stands of balsam
especially in winter,
Vermont is everyone's America,
my wreath a token from
the country of my heart.

<151>

Lake Tear of the Clouds

Hard to imagine
in the far Adirondacks
Lake Tear of the Clouds
gives birth to this giant.

I sit beside the shore
listen to the lapping waves.
Warblers flit about
in the sedge grass.
Above the Palisades
the sky is lemon yellow.
A drift of smoke
among the pine trees
is consumed in the evening air.

Here, where the river is widest,
boats sail up
and down the stream.
I imagine the water journey
up river towards Albany
under the ramparts of Storm King
and then, beyond Lake George,
that smaller river
a thin blue line on maps —
that leads to the little lake,
Lake Tear of the Clouds.

All our beginnings are small.

<152>

Diner

Boonville, NY

I sat in a diner
up in Boonville.
Outside woods flamed
in the October landscape.
Harvest time was over.

The man beside me
was eating soup —
strong brown hands
clutched the spoon
as if it were to dig with.

We got to talking:
Great weather.
Is the harvest in?
Innocent eyes
blue as the sky,
a quiff of sandy hair.

Going south to look for work.
Nothing up here.
Laid the spoon down
gently in the plate.

<153>

Sense of Place

Weary of the sounds
from the streets
no escaping the
assaults on the spirit
the wail of sirens
the cacophony of sounds
calculated to destroy equilibrium
no center can hold
against this intrusion

A beloved book sheds
comfort from its pages
the daily progress
of a writer's life
in an old stone house
near the Adirondacks

The simple details
of his search
for the showy lady slipper
changes in the weather
behavior of linnets,
the ways of a wintry people.

Something immutable
in this recording
of small events
creates a peaceful
sense of place.

<154>

Retreat

Reading three papers
fills my mind with jumbled images,
makes me feel the world
is too much to handle.

I retreat —
read a much-loved book
by a writer in upstate New York
just diary entries —
the daily progress of his life
in his old stone house
years ago.

After this
I feel a calm sense
that maybe, just maybe
there is still someone, some place
writing like this,
perhaps Bob Stauder
in the Catskills.

<155>

Vision Quest

In memoriam — Edmund Wilson

Sometimes my world
is too much to handle —
There's no escape
from the jarring sounds
in urban streets —
my spirit cannot hold to center.

I turn to a much-loved book —
the daily progress of a writer's life
in an old stone house
near the Adirondacks.
He wrote of the showy lady slipper,
a local flower,
and the changing seasons in the hills;
the ways of country people
and the ever-changing weather.

<156>

Upstate

This town is old and small,
bounded by open country.
Fields stripped of harvest,
forests are ablaze with color;
the scent of wood smoke
permeates the air.

On Main Street scarlet leaves
scatter to the pavements,
rustle softly in the white gazebo
on the village green.
A distant sound of music —
they're line dancing
at the inn tonight.

They circle and turn
in the big old room.
Filled with quiet confidence,
they celebrate community.
Dusk closes in on the town.
Footsteps resonate
in the silence.

Nothing spectacular.
Lives in harmony with the seasons,
here the center holds.
That's how it is,
this October evening,
a small town near the Sugar River,
west of the Adirondacks.

<157>

Tappan Zee

Today, God's spirit
shone forth
by the rolling river
the trees, emblazoned
with autumn
riotous with color
and the sea gulls
beloved, a blessing
on the Tappan Zee
the sky, a royal blue
banner
and the glorious sun
striking sparkles from
the water.
There is nothing left
to do, my love —
but tell you about this
and make the telling of
this marvelous day
my evening prayer
and wish you had been there.

<158>

George Washington, If You Could See Your Bridge

You would turn to Martha
In wonderment and say,
"Gee, Martha, who's the guy
who named this noisy link of steel
in remembrance of me?

"I always was a quiet man, Martha.
I never had much to say
even when we chased the British
not saying much I had my way.

"I suppose I should be proud, Martha
of this humongous traffic way
and think of all the folks it serves —
every blooming day."

<159>

The Diadems of the Hudson

I

You are immense
A creation in iron and steel
Your green and gold lights reflected
in the gray waters of the river

How vulnerable you are
oh mighty bridge
the chain that links us to the
great metropolis

Your towers —
sentinels above the river
gleaming against the sky
gray with rain clouds

I want to protect you
against those ...
for you represent
an emblem

Your lights glisten like crystal on
traffic streaming to the city
from our suburban enclave.

II

You span history
the great river flows under
your highways
and the folks cross you
to and fro, day and night.
Who thinks of how vulnerable you are?

As I look at you
dark clouds from the west
cross the sky.
Is this an omen?

<160>

Aftermath

For Peter,
thirteen weeks at
Ground Zero

You told me
working in the ruins
of those toppled giants
your spirits were lifted
by the men of Idaho,
California, Wisconsin —
all, like so many others,
come to render help.

You told me
the folks you worked with
side by side, faces set
in determined energy,
did what had to be done
under the banners
made by children
in our nation's schools —
alive with messages of love.

You told me
now you see people smile
at one another,
greet strangers as they would a friend.
And when those great beams of light
soared into the night
you told me you saw America
unvanquished.

<161>

NY Man

I remember the first time
I saw you
(saw pictures but the
reality moved me more
than I can say)
that day on Fort Tryon Park
chickadee on my hand
below the slow flowing river
across from us the high palisades
people strolling on the paths
and all around the busy city
strange and yet familiar
full of possibilities

<162>

Moment in Midtown

Near the bus station
on 42nd Street
he lay, in the fetal position
hands neatly joined between
his knees

somebody's son from somewhere
given up, can't hack it
anymore.

on his cheek, a thin line of blood
his heart beating a
faint flicker of life
in an abandoned (moment)

in his clenched hand
someone had put
a single dollar bill

<163>

New York City

Walking through those great stone canyons
I lift my face to feel the faint sea breeze
Blown upwards from the narrows
over the steely Verrazano.

I see, over the rim of the tall buildings,
more buildings, soaring upwards,
giving back, glassily,
the muted pink of evening sky.

And along the cobbled sidewalks, by Central Park,
mini-skirted girls, offices, a solitary stride.

<164>

Miss Holybrooke in Central Park

Miss Holybrooke
sits in the park,
her broad-brimmed hat
with its nodding rose
frames her eighty-year-old face,
remnants of prettiness
caught in a web of wrinkles,
eyes blue as grape hyacinths.

She smiles vaguely,
watches the roller-bladers
skim by, ears sealed by head-sets.
They do not smile —
earnest, self-absorbed,
what do they know of the tune
Miss Holybrooke hums
from Nineteen Thirty-Five?

Skaters whirl around
inexorable as time
measured by a ticking clock.
A sudden October breeze
sends leaves fluttering.
One falls on the brim
of Miss Holybrooke's hat,
a companion to her rose.

The air turns chill,
wind sends a shower of leaves
onto the footpath.
They rustle like little ghosts
in the twilight.
Miss Holybrooke rises,
walks slowly under the trees,
her small shape diminishing
in the fading light.

<165>

Mr. Meyer at Coney Island

Mr. Meyer sits on the boardwalk,
his eighty-year-old face
a web of wrinkles,
crowned by silver hair.
He surveys the Atlantic.
Behind him, the Parachute Jump
a spidery silhouette
against the evening sky.

He thinks about the towers,
minarets and spires,
lights blazing like diamonds,
and the girl he met there,
red-haired, eyes blue
as grape hyacinths.
What was her name?
He can't recall.

He hears the gulls' cries,
remembers the screams
of the red-haired girl,
hugged in his arms
as the roller coaster
plunged down the wooden tracks.
Now, in a more perilous world,
such thrills seem tame.

He recites in his mind
the magical litany of names:
Steeplechase, Luna Park,
Dreamland, Cyclone,
Nathan's nickel hot dog.
For him, Coney Island
is a place of nostalgia,
a world of dreams and shadows.

<166>

Mr. Meyer rises;
the evening is chill.
He walks towards Brighton Beach,
hears only the resonance
of the rolling waves,
and the gulls' distant cries.
And he sighs for his
lost Coney Island.

<167>

Jersey Trails

Aug 2005 — Riegelsville, PA

Trees sigh in a breeze
from the west —
through the woods
the rounded shoulders
of the Appalachians are
blue in the distance
the sky, now another
shade of blue,
now evening.

White clouds float
cast shadows
about the rural landscape
green as emeralds.

In the shed two men
are repairing a machine
their slow hammer blows
accompanied by the distant
engine of a plane.

Far out in this
verdant countryside
away from the town
hurly-burly
I find tranquillity —
I'm in another world.

<171>

Highlands

For Stefan

Frozen earth crunches
beneath our footsteps,
the quick fluttering of
juncos in the greenbriar
makes a small stir,
surrounding us
the sharp smell
of clean Highland air.

In these silent woods
streams murmur
below a filigree of ice,
oak leaves, autumn's ghosts
rimed with frost
carpet the ground,
the red of osiers
winter's ruddy boat.

We hike up Hamburg Mountain,
our window to the endless view:
in the distance, High Point
extends a finger to the sky,
the Kittatinny ridge
in the west
a heart-wrenching blue
in the evening light.

In the ring of winter
on this wooded spine
of New Jersey,
no sound
but the sighing wind,
and we have found
tranquility
walking the high ground.

<172>

A Jersey Welcome

From the window
I see two women
in the bitter cold
weave Christmas lights,
green and gold,
through the evergreens
along the railing
of the old hotel.

They have a reason —
there should be
a cheerful welcome
at the Holy Season.

They stand
in the frigid air
hands clasped as if in prayer,
waiting for the twinkle
that tells travelers
who come from near and far,
they have arrived
at the Inn.

The lights gleam,
the women smile —
their faces shine
like the Christmas star.

This poem was published under the alternate title of "In Ogdensburg."

<173>

Sept 22 — Sussex Branch, Augusta to Branchville

name blue flowers
   yellow
     thistles   purples

Lehigh and New England
rough trail
one main line to
carry coal to New England
abandoned 1961

crickets
meadow gone fallow
meadow hay
cows once grazed
milk to
dairy once
on the Lackawanna

rabbit ears
fields of corn
leaves already
turning
old moss covered ties
cinder path
passing dry brook
trees reflected in
water

little rough
good for horses
dry branch
about 3/4 mile up
path washed out
go carefully

<174>

heron sunning on
rock
rills on the dry brook
glimmer in
sun

railroad ended 1966
commuter line
in later years
new growth forest
stream fast flowing
sound of water rushing
hiking to Branchville
passing under Route 15
Queen Anne's Lace
smoke from long
past steam locomotive
darkened the
girders of the
bridge.

crossed over
brook to
Branchville
Milk Street.
3 miles total.

<175>

The Paulinskill Valley Trail

Sussex County

Follow your way westwards
to where the Paulins Kill[1] flows.
Follow the winding valley trail
by meadows and by woods,
listen to the bird song
and the whispering stream
bounded by the Kittatinnies,
a Lenape name from long ago.
From Augusta to Columbia
at first a modest flow;
by the trail beneath the mountains
the river deepens as it goes.

Here the Jersey countryside
is peaceful and serene,
a place of silence and tranquility,
a place to sit and dream.

---

[1] The Paulins Kill was called by the Indians *Tockhockonetcong.*

<176>

Waiting for Stef in Blairstown

I sit on a bench in Blairstown
a place in West Jersey
unchanged and beautiful —
waiting for you to join me.

I think about our hike
on the Paulinskill Valley Trail
and our drive from the little airport
to this most charming town.

Blairstown, a place of some renown,
named for a generous American
many years ago.
I will be slow to lose the memory
of that day in Blairstown —
a little town in West Jersey
unchanged through the years
beautiful in the old American way.

<177>

Hiking the Lockwood Gorge

Frozen earth crunches
beneath our footsteps,
the quiet whisper of the Raritan
below our path.
Juncos in the greenbrier
make a small stir
surrounding us
the sharp smell
of fresh December air.

In the silent woods
streams
above the trees
in their winter loneliness,
the sky, a frigid blue.
Only the crows calling
breaks the silence
until, down the path,
a man and two boys
come toward us,
laughter ringing out.
Twin boys in red jackets
and caps like pixies
laugh as they race about.

<178>

Hiking the Columbia Trail

Mist drifts in the winter trees,
a little chill in the air.
Just enough to keep us going,
hiking the trail
to Lockwood Gorge.

A thin sprinkle of snow
hushes our footsteps.
Far below the river flows
southwards to the Bay.
Ahead the high cliffs of the Gorge,
trees growing out of rocky crevices.
The Gorge, a Hunterdon marvel.

In the distance, voices.
Down the path two little boys
come running, tumbling, giggling,
their red caps and jackets
rosy lanterns in the misty air.
Their father, out of breath,
halts their onward rush.

We smile in their antics,
young ones in the winter woods,
denizens of this special corner
of New Jersey.
As we pass they joyfully chirp
"You have a nice day."

A variation of "Hiking the Lockwood Gorge."

<179>

Clinton Furnace (Early Version)

Only the rushing torrent now
Fills the air with sounds
Where the great bellows roared
Feeding the flames in the furnace.

Clinton Furnace is a place lost to memory
As secretive as a Mayan ruin
Deep in the Jersey Woods.

Stone on unmortared stone
The furnace stands, a monument
To the nameless miners
Who brought the crushed stone to the furnace
On ships pulled by mules
through the Jersey woods.

<180>

Clinton Furnace

A lost place in the Jersey woods
mysterious as a Mayan ruin
the old furnace
heavy unmortared stone
by the rushing torrent
here they made pig iron.

Hard to imagine the hills
one hundred years ago
bare summits, scarified.
Now, in the leafy shade
only the rushing torrent
tumbling among the stones.

Here the great bellows roared.
Mules hauled ore to the canal.
Men clambered to feed
the furnace.

<181>

Autumn Rapture — Clinton, NJ

That October day we stood,
three of us by the Raritan River,
you and I and a young boy
watching a fisherman
cast his line below the rush
of the spillway.

The boy told us a story.
He had caught a carp.
"This long..." he said,
holding his arms wide,
an exaggerated gesture,
drawing our astonished praise.

The trees on the limestone cliffs
wore their Autumn color,
families strolled across the bridge
to the old Red Mill,
its great water wheel a symbol
of a long ago time.

Downstream the fisherman
reeled in his catch,
his line a curl of silver in the sunlight.
The boy grinned a smile
of knowing satisfaction.

Something to hold on to:
your hand in mine,
a happy boy, a fisherman rewarded,
the sound of distant laughter,
a Sunday in October
by the surging Raritan River.

<182>

Jersey Day

There is magic in Long Valley.
Driving past fields, emerald green,
and the sweet houses
of the Jersey countryside,
we are going to the inn.
Here and there a red barn
and the soft sweep of the hills.
In little towns antique shops
hold treasures from long ago.
At the inn there's cheery friendship,
the hum of happy voices.
There's something special here,
a sense of Jersey hospitality.
Evening as we leave the Valley
two children wave by the roadside,
their handwrought sign says
"Iced Tea" and "Lemonade."
We stop and taste their offerings.
The boy whistles cheerfully,
the girl gently smiles.
Then we go on our way,
a perfect ending to a Jersey day.

<183>

Ballooning

A silent drifting
wallowing in air
over country
autumn clad
elephantine shapes
in a sky
turquoise blue
float up
above the many colored
crowd
exhaling in wonder —
a faint hissing
says good-bye

<184>

Hunterdon Hackberry[2]

You stand, brave old tree,
a challenge to history.
The shadows of your gnarled limbs
stretch across daisy-starred grass,
twisted branches reach to the sky.
There is a solemnity about you.
Were you witness to the labors
of our early settlers —
to our heroes marching to battle
two hundred years ago?
In the waning light of evening
I salute you.
Bereft of many branches
there is nothing sad about you.
May you long stand proudly,
a testament to history —
our New Jersey sentinel.

---

[2] The 300-year-old Hunterdon Hackberry stands on private land in Hunterdon.
It is the oldest tree in the county. In diameter it is 19 feet 6 inches.

<185>

Fragment of a Villanelle

Walking in the cemetery today
I notice Autumn's colors on the trees
Signals of the season on the way

Over the Ramapos the sky is gray
Distant birdsong on a gentle breeze
Walking in the cemetery today

Soon I'll see the Autumn's full display
Across the valley and the far-off fields
Signals of the season on the way

I do not feel in any sense dismay
I know that Summer's sun to Autumn yields
Walking in the cemetery today
Signals of the season on the way.

The completed version of this poem is in Volume 2.

<186>

Hiking the Old Lackawanna

The woods are a thousand
shades of brown,
winter grass a deep amber.
Lit by the sun's golden rays
ice-covered pools of
the Black River
shine like silver.

In the woods
crows are calling
and down the trail
a dog barks warning.
Here the Black River
meanders,
forms pools now
glazed with winter ice
shining like silver
in the setting sun.

Over the trees the sky
a frigid blue.
A few stray clouds
white as the snow
on our path
drifts towards the west.

Down the path
running, to you.

<187>

A Meaning Beyond Expected Explanations

Behind me the highway
filled with a noise of traffic
Before me the rise

The trees, in full leaf
rise against a pale blue sky
flutter in the spring sky
breeze
majestic against a pale
blue sky

Here in the center of NJ
I am nearer to the
essence of nature
the sense of the eternal
beauty in nature
that fills my soul
with ecstasy.
The strength and beauty of
trees
marvels of creation
I seek in this beauty
a meaning beyond accepted
explanations.

<188>

A Peaceful Place

Do you know Quakertown?
Go there in early spring
when the trees and hedges
come into leaf.
One day I walked around
this quiet, small place
where the past lives on
in the Quaker names
of the old graveyard.

I watched a farmer heave
bales of straw from his barn.
Wide fields stretch away,
a peaceful pattern to the West.
Nothing spectacular —
just a small American town.
To walk there in Spring
and breathe the sweet air
refreshes the spirit.

In the distance a line of hills,
blue on the horizon.
A man came bicycling by,
greeted me cheerfully.
"What is the name of those hills?" I asked.
"Those," he said, wrinkling his forehead.
"Why, Ma'am, those are the blue hills
of Hunterdon County."
I went on my way, satisfied.

<189>

Jersey Shore (A Thought)

A pier
is a
frustrated
bridge?

<190>

The Source

The narrow stream
glimmers under brambles
a smell of moist humus
sharp on the air
in the undergrowth
a bell-like tinkle.

This little drift
of water
holds promises
standing in the wood.
I listen to its quiet
whispering
over wet stones.

At this gentle source
of the Passaic
it is hard to imagine
in the flute-voiced water
the thundering falls
at Paterson.

<191>

New Bridge

The disheartened army
tramping down the
winding roads
from the precipice

<192>

Hackensack

Down by the Hackensack
a little silver moon
and a train whistle
sounding
as Conrail proceeds north
through the town
the iron rattle of its wheels
dying in the distance
and a silver moon shining
on the river as it flows
slowly past the Steuben House
small sounds of lapping
water near the old bridge

<193>

Ghosts

It is evening at New Bridge —
someone in the Steuben House
carries a light from room to room.
It flickers as it goes from
window to window.

The swift-flowing waters
of the Hackensack lap the shore.
It is strangely quiet by the river.
Only a far away hum of traffic
breaks the silence.
Standing on the Bridge
I try to imagine the men
marching from Fort Lee
crossing the Hackensack in '76.

Loving couple, hand in hand
come down the old road way,
come across the bridge.
They talk and laugh quietly as they pass.
Was it for this that the generals'
troops fought?

<194>

At the Steuben House

Like a cello, softly played
protectively,
I stand on the bridge.

In the setting sun trees cast soft shadows
on the slow-flowing Hackensack.
Candlelight winks out in the old house.

Somewhere in the distance a dog barks.
A boy's voice calls like a distant bugle.
High above, a plane flies over Bergen County.

A loving couple, hand in hand,
slowly cross the old bridge,
their voices only a murmur.

Was it for this the soldiers marched
that long ago day in 1776?
Carrying with them freedom for America?

<195>

Cemetery Trio

1
The orderly rows terraced
on the hillside
who knows now who
they were
I come here for comfort
The men are always
working here —
I hear their machines
hum and throb
as they garden
among the graves
I would like to ask them
"Do you ponder on your
fate — someday to rest here?"
but I'm afraid of their replies

2
Now the newly fallen snow
caps the granite stones —
no one soul here do I know
or knows me
but I share with humanity the
same, irrevocable fate
why then be afraid —
on this sloping hillside
bathed in winter sunshine
the whitened graves
are a comfort —
this is our ungathering
of the dead
hallowed ground
and as I turn to leave
silently the first flakes of
snow begin to gently fall
on

<196>

3
Under this coverlet
of snow
the unimpeachable dead
sleep in neat orderly rows.
At each head, a stone
bearing a name and date
nothing of the fate
which brought them
here — I mean
to this far land —
wait — I find, in a
sheltered corner
— from Co. Clare.
Am I the only one, I wonder
who lingers there —
pondering on the journey
across three thousand miles
of ocean
to the new land, after all
the date is —
America then was only —

<197>

Looking for Pop's Grave[3]

headstones
names
stones on top
sun
warm
aisle of trees
distant sound of traffic
figure walking
between headstones
looking seeking searching
for Pop's grave
old link with Russia
never close
no closer now than
then
when he was here — alive
I follow you, their son
through aisles of stones
older now than when
your mother died

---

[3] "Pop" was Jack Bailis's father, who died around age 93. His mother died in
1952, age 52, of breast cancer.

<198>

Gulls in Little Ferry

On the parking lot
the gulls come
beseeching me
fox-like and
their shrill cries
rise over Valley Fair
the spring air
is filled with the flashing
of their wings

I go down there
by the slow-flowing Hackensack
every so often
to show them
I remember they are
there
in from the sea
they shout
Hosannaon
when I come
catching bits of bread
with a quick turn of their heads.
I feel it a privilege
to satisfy
their voracious need.

<199>

Hudson

We sit beside
the slow moving river
inexorable
that elemental force
thrusting towards the sea.
We do not speak
listen only to the wind
in the rusty reeds
the warblers' small cries
in the dogwoods
bare now of leaves.
We are lulled
by this timeless flow
behind us.
Above the Palisades
a wisp of smoke
blue against a lemon sky
goes skyward through the trees
ephemeral
a counterpoint to
the fluvial force
ever flowing, flowing
southwards to the sea.

<200>

Fort Lee Journeys

Winter Stroll, Fort Lee

These flakes like falling feathers
Drift softly down on Fort Lee's streets.
Overhead, a cold gray sky
Stretching to the Kittatinnies
Gives me sign of better weather.
Soon this town of ours will struggle
With this symbol of cold days
lying in heaps on our pavements
blocking our busy pedestrian ways.

Main Street, Fort Lee

On Main Street
I can hear the sound of
country music.
The air smells of wood smoke.
A bright new moon
shines above the roof tops.

It is peaceful here.
Red and gold leaves
pattern the pavements.
The white gazebo is ghostlike
in the village green.

<203>

At the Diner

In the warmth
of the diner
the group
chatted —
laughter rose
and fell
magnified
in the empty
space —
the chink of spoons
against coffee cups
made a kind of music —

a gaunt man
sad-eyed
entered —
watched in
amazement
as a couple
rose and
cut loose
down the aisle
in a fantastic tango
celebrating life.

<204>

Irish Voices

In the busy restaurant
I see three people
sitting in a corner
quietly chatting.
Something familiar about them
something in the way they sit, close,
talking in low voices.

I go over.
Irish voices —

and holding out his hand
the young man says "Slán abhaile."

I watch them
try to catch
some remark,
some hint of place.

<205>

Ordinary Noises

hammer
train whistle
police car
fire truck

and the bird-like voices of
children coming home from
school
flurry of pigeons wing
across the yard
the drone of a plane
sometimes in the distance
a droning sound
an urgent calling
is it an alarm or simply
have an old significance
like the bells on lighthouses
standing near lonely shores

the thump of rock from
a passing van
driven by an earnest teenager
giggling at the wheel

sounds of everyday
much as a landscape
evokes the past to the initiate
so these sounds evoke
the living

<206>

Four Haiku

Evening shadows fall ...
In tall trees shrill cicadas
Cacophonous call

Dare I ask the tree
To whisper its green secrets
To my waiting ear?

One purple Iris
lone in a shadowed corner
Makes a brave statement

A gentle Spring breeze ...
Memorial flags flutter
On ancestors' graves

<207>

Hero[1]

Standing by your grave
I read your name, so simple,
James Conway, died at Antietam
Twenty years of age.

Who were you, James,
Soldier and hero.
What were your hopes and aspirations?
At twenty life opens up before us
Filled with promise.
But you went South, James,
Firmly to defend the Union.

In the cemetery trees
The soft calling of a mourning dove.
We must not mourn for you, James,
Only salute you, dead 142 years.
We will praise you
With respect and love,
Son of the Republic.

---

[1] Moira Bailis rediscovered the grave of James Conway at Madonna Cemetery in
Fort Lee, NJ, prompting its rededication by the town's VFW post.

<208>

Alone in the Cemetery

Between the sides of tombs
a rabbit runs as
the breeze from the west
stirs the maples,
sets flags dancing.
The air is full of murmurs.

On O'Grady's tomb
Born County Clare, Ireland
a robin perches,
flies off on my approach
draws a thread of sweet music
down the hillside.

I fancy I hear
O'Grady's Irish brogue
on the wind
and Mary Moore's from Athenry
and the Polish mazurkas
of the Wieniawskis.

Marcantonio's canzone
seems to soar in the air,
lyrical chansons
from the Renans of France,
lieder from the Hausmanns.

The voices of Fort Lee's
"glorious resurrected"
join in triumphant
Hallelujahs.
Surrounded by their presence
I start singing
alone
in the cemetery.

<209>

Tohmey

Light gilds the tops of
tombstones — monuments
In the western sky
setting sun sets the clouds
on fire
Trees cast long shadows
on the grass, green as
emerald
Above me the old church
with beckoning spire
raised to the evening sky
caressed by the rays
of the setting sun.
Peace. God is here.
In the distance the
Ramapos misty blue
Down in the valley
the distant rumble
of traffic.
Cross raised against the
sky
The gold of the setting sun
a patina
on the old stone
There is no sadness here
Among the holy dead.
God is Here.
mauve hills
gold ring of the sun
church a guardian
over all this beauty.

<210>

Lights flashing in the valley
In the tree a robin call
Flags rustle in a light
breeze from the west
Irish Polish German
Italian
the names of Europe
engraved in stone

<211>

The Church on the Hill

Above me the old church
Caressed by the rays
Of the setting sun
Its beckoning spire
Raised to the evening sky —
A monument to faith.

The gold of the sunrays
Gilds the tops of tombstones,
the names; a roll call
of Fort Lee history.
Across the valley the Ramapos
A wall of gentle blue.

A breeze comes from the West.
In the trees a mourning dove calls.
The old church stands, a blessing
On this peaceful place.
There is no sadness here —
This is sacred ground.

Tonight

The face of the moon is dark tonight
We watched, standing in the church yard
As the first pale shadow crept upwards
Slowly bringing a pink glow to the
brilliant light.

<212>

Shadows

In the dim hall of the cathedral
a meager group
filters up the aisle
to the sanctuary
where the candles glow.
Hollow sounds — street sounds
filter through
the red-robed choir
in calm deliberation
files to the nave
chants psalms which
echo to the roof tops
cold despairing — all the
woes of mankind centered
in sufferings of Jesus,
the hard floor under knees.

One by one candles extinguished
choir files out — last candle
taken behind altar.
Chastened, in silence,
the congregants
file into the darkness
leaving the steady light
of this single candle
to console the human heart.

And this last light —
small as the last flicker of life
the last faltering breath
vanishes behind the altar as
woeful darkness descends.

<213>

The Eve of Christmas

Sunset colors the sky.
In the valley of the Hackensack
festive lights glow and twinkle
from Fort Lee's highest point.
I look out over this corner
of beloved America
in this season of celebration.

Yet a thought enters my mind
when so many are joined
in joyful anticipation —
What of the lost and homeless?
The poor and suffering?
Our soldiers far from home?
I am confronted by the mystery
of human existence —
I ask, what is the answer?

Far away a bell softly tolls,
a thought comes to mind.
Long, long ago in distant Bethlehem
a simple manger,
a little child
bringing a message —
"love one another,"
a consolation to the world.
My question answered
as the sails of faith unfurl.

<214>

Simplicity

A resonating sound
goes down my street,
tells me that Julia
is coming home from school.
She walks along
with slow feet,
she doesn't see me
waiting by the hedge.
Keeping a measured beat
she earnestly taps
her basketball.
The pleasures of a little girl
are very small.

<215>

The Bike

There it is
chained
near the school wall —
an eight year old's bike.
It is red,
cherry red
chrome gleaming.
Its license plate reads
Robert.
Its rider,
forehead creased,
bound to his desk,
puts his trust in chains
while he learns to spell
"b-i-c-y-c-l-e".

<216>

Walking — A Prose Poem

Walking has been one of the joys of my life. The air, cool on my cheeks, refreshes me. I stand still and watch the birds fluttering in the spring trees. Above me a plane flies over to Teterboro — I imagine folks filled with joy on trips home.

One day I walked a few miles, an energetic spring in my step, greeted by friendly passersby; despite my weight of years, I am filled with happiness. When folks smile and say "Hi" there is a sense of companionship.

This particular day I walked two miles, arrived filled with a sense of achievement. I stood before my son's house, looking at his flowering spring garden.
A door opened and out he came — his face a mix of anxiety and curiosity. He asked, in tones of reproach — "*You* walked all the way *here*?"

<217>

To an Irish Friend

When you get to Fort Lee
turn south from the bridge
along Lemoine Ave
the trafficked street —
past an island of greenery
down to where all
widens out by a little mall.
Turn right and pass the school.
Perhaps young Fort Lee will be
leaving for the day —
if so, the street will be clogged.

Go slowly past the
1940s houses with trim yards
until you see a shady park
in which stands a lone fireman,
his statue commemorating our hero.

Turn left, with care
children skateboard here.
Up ahead, three huge boulders
mark a dead end —
one more left onto my street,
a little street of Cape Cod houses.
Perhaps you will meet
a neighbor, dog walking
or a boy on a bicycle
tooling along.
It's a safe street,
only fourteen houses
built sixty years ago.

<218>

Behind a thicket of greenery
I will wait for you.
We will sit on my patio
where the fountain tinkles
and drink tea from green cups
that will remind you
of Ireland.

<219>

No Words Suffice

Words have no limits
for me to describe
a longing
for this kind of life.
I think, with age
one longs for certainties,
to be one with the
line dancers.

Walking home through the
tranquil town
kicking the autumn leaves
something of that town's
tranquillity
enters my room
as I write —

There's another dimension
to memory —
in that a small town
must give a sense of place.

<220>

New House

It looms over the hedges
with a barracks-like air.
It cuts off the light
of the setting sun.

My son tells me not to care,
it is the way things are now.
Ostentation rules.
My home is small, New Englandy
built on this little street
sixty years ago.

I listen to the sound of hammers
all day a steady beat.
I find it hard to be unaware
of what is coming:
all our houses out of style now.

They pulled down the old house
yellow brick nineteen forties
once home to a good friend.

<221>

Mornings on Abbott

The cherries are in bloom again
On Abbott Boulevard —
Their rosy blossoms pink
Above grass, green as emeralds.
They make a statement —
Spring is here.

The cottonwoods flourish —
A fresh breeze from the South
Sets their leaves dancing.
The warm brick of a 1940s house,
its garden a riot of color,
vies with the red of Japanese maples.

Here citizens stroll or jog —
Greet me cheerfully —
It's a way of life in Fort Lee.
I turn for home, happy.
Another morning Abbott stroll
Has set my spirit free.

<222>

Ode

This corner of the world
smiles for me beyond
    all

<223>

Chair Mirror Window Sky

Sitting in my easy chair
before the window,
a mirror for the evening sky —
I try to see beauty in day's end.
I don't know why.

<224>

Nail

For want of a nail
my old dresser sags
filled with mementos
of long ago.
I am aware of its presence
but that is all.
I never open its drawers
never polish its wooden surface
with loving care.
It stands there
like a memorial to childhood
long passed but never
forgotten.

<225>

Cleaning House

It takes a while to consider
where to start.
My house is small
but even so, it's a chore.
I dress for the occasion —
an old housedress
from twenty years ago
and the blue Irish cardigan.
That's my uniform for the job.
So outfitted, it comes easier,
the lifting, bending, stretching.

While the vacuum hums
over the carpets,
I sing along with
old songs of the Forties,
"Singin' in the Rain,"
"Deep in the Heart of Texas."
The rhythm suits my push and pull
as I go from room to room.

Soon things begin to shine,
order is restored.
The gleam of sunshine on a
polished floor
lifts my spirits.
I breathe lemon-scented air.
I change my tune,
sing out "'Tis a gift to be simple."
I wonder why I feel
such a sense of satisfaction —
then decide — a job well done
is its own reward.

<226>

Back Yard

My shirts on the line
open parachutes
in windy weather.

The back fence leans in
shadows the growing tulips.
No more yellow and red.

The slender lodge pole pines
stand so close together
a wall of privacy.

Look like drunks at a funeral.

<227>

Habitat

When I open the door
something happens —
it is as if the house
welcomes me.
A feeling. "Home."
What does that mean?
I walk from room to room.
In my kitchen each cup, each plate,
each pot and dish holds a story
a link through years of happiness,
family celebrations, holidays
and holy days.
That tea pot poured for my
mother, twenty-five years ago
her last visit to America.
And there's the candle holder
a gift from my daughter-in-law
on a birthday.
The familiar objects
connect events in a long life
each having a story,
point to a continuum.
I look at the old table
marked by our four pairs of hands
and the cats' begging scratches,
the comforting familiarity of it all.

<228>

Dandelion

One dandelion
manicured suburban lawn
Nature's optimist

<229>

Creeper

My son says, pull
that out
before it takes over
the whole yard.
I look at the green
gray tendrils
the little, sprightly leaves
the berries red as
good wine —

My friend, a Friend,
says —
We hate that creeper,
it takes over the whole
place
where we meet on
Sundays —

I say to myself —
anything hated as this
deserves to live.

I'll let it live.

<230>

Coda:
The Antidote
To Prejudice

Righteous People

People who are self-righteous, self-opinionated.
Do you know the sort of people that I mean?
They've all the answers
never an in-between

but absolutely black or white
their answers are
no matter what the subject should be.
Peace or *war*.

They know everything
and understand nothing.

"Travel is fatal to prejudice, bigotry, and narrow-mindedness, and many of our people need it sorely on these accounts. Broad, wholesome, charitable views of men and things cannot be acquired by vegetating in one little corner of the Earth all of one's lifetime."

— Mark Twain, Conclusion
Innocents Abroad: or, The New Pilgrim's Progress (1869).

<233>

AFTERWORD

MOIRA BAILIS is one of the few living poets in the United States to write poems in nine different decades (an achievement also made by Stanley Kunitz, who wrote between 1928 and 2006). Her earliest poem is "9 Sept 1939" (written on that date, at the age of 18), and her latest poem is "Outback" (a "found poem" culled from a 2010 conversation). These are two of the 190 poems that grace *The Antidote to Prejudice*, the first of a two-volume set of *Collected Poems of Moira Bailis*. This and the second volume, a 260-poem collection titled *It Has To Do With Seeing*, are scheduled for publication on her 90th birthday in late February 2011. Between the two volumes, over 200 never-before-seen poems will make their public debut.

The Antidote to Prejudice celebrates 75 years of travel, from her first trip at the age of 15 to her local journeys these days in the town of Fort Lee, New Jersey, where she has lived since January 1, 1966. "Travel is fatal to prejudice, bigotry, and narrowmindedness," said Mark Twain, in 1869 — a remark that retains heightened relevance today, in our world of increasing polarization, self-centeredness, righteousness, and intolerance. *It Has to Do With Seeing* clusters additional poems thematically, and also includes early and variant texts.

Moira started life in Ireland in 1921, lived in Europe in the 1950s, moved to the United States in the 1960s, and over the course of her life traveled across four continents: North America, Europe, Asia, and Australia. Poems that could be perceived as capturing the spirit or essence of South America, Africa, and even Antarctica were selected and arranged to round out Volume 1.

When anyone reaches age 90 or higher, like it or not, he or she becomes "living history." Thus, many of her poems — especially in the Ireland section — are dually interesting from the standpoints of poetic craft and the capturing of history, from "On Seeing Maud Gonne, Dublin 1942" to "The Last Tram, November 1949."

Moira crossed paths with a lot of interesting people — no surprise, considering her early background as a journalist. Some of these encounters inspired interesting poems, while some parts of her personal history were never captured in poetry (such as the time she was the personal tour guide for Ralph Ellison in Germany, shortly after publication of *Invisible Man*). Personal encounters with Maud Gonne, Patrick Kavanagh, Sheelagh Kirby, Joseph Brodsky, James Merrill, and more are among the finds within the two-volume set.

While Moira was extensively published in my publication, *Sensations Magazine*, across two decades, her work also appeared in other literary

<235>

magazines and publications both in the United States and Ireland, including *Appalachian Journal*, *Contemporary Review*, *Irish Voice*, *Journal of Irish Literature*, *Parnassus*, *Poet Magazine*, and others listed in the Publication Credits section.

Many poets hinge their careers on whom they've met and where they've published. More important to Moira, however, is the attempt to create art through poetry, to share and impart knowledge, and to find beauty — whether in a person, place, thing, or the world at large. She also doesn't shy away from outlining evil, or examining and chronicling intolerance and injustice, as poems such as *"Wir hatten uns gefürchtet..."* and "Mississippi Death Trip" strongly show.

Throughout her life, and into today, Moira would strike up a conversation with a complete stranger, and utilize that opportunity to learn about that person's language, culture, background, ideals, and dreams. Some of the poems in this collection derive from that process, and we all benefit from the results.

I chose a thematic sequencing of Moira's poetry for the two-volume set. Moira did not date many of her poems, so a straight chronological sequencing of 450 pieces written across nine decades is impossible (though I will take a stab at creating a researched chronology of her poetry in the near future). All of the poems published in her now out-of-print 2003 chapbook *poems* (ISBN 0967-6066-9-1) are republished across the two-volume set, incorporating edits that she wanted included. All of her poems previously published in magazines in the United States and Ireland are republished as well. If you purchase both volumes, 98% of her lifetime of poetry writing will be in your hands.

Moira was strongly engaged in the American poetry scene for over 20 years. She worked at her poetry, rewriting and revising frequently to get each poem to the best level she could. Unlike many American poets, she occasionally wrote in form; her efforts at haiku, acrostic, villanelle, and in meter and rhyme are among these published works.

Moira attended writing workshops offered through the Main Street Poets in Fort Lee, NJ; she also was a member of the North River Poets, the Saturday Afternoon Poets, the New Jersey Poetry Society, and the League of Minnesota Poets. She was a featured reader in many poetry series in New Jersey, reading at independent bookstores, libraries, and museums. As a wide-ranging scholar, she researched and lectured on Chinese, Irish, Jewish, and Russian poets, as well as other writers ("The Poetry of James Joyce," "Shakespeare's Irish Connection") and other topics (*e.g.*, the American Labor Movement, Sacco and Vanzetti). She co-hosted a monthly poetry radio show, "The Poet's Corner," on Sunday mornings on WFDU-FM from 1996 to 2007. As a volunteer, she taught English to Korean

<236>

students in Fort Lee and, starting in 1986, held annual children's poetry workshops at Fort Lee Public Library during National Library Week.

While researching and securing the manuscript for this book, we uncovered personal letters to her by Joseph Parisi, famed editor of *Poetry Magazine*. She also corresponded with Kathryn Stripling Byer, Poet Laureate of North Carolina (in her book, *Black Shawl*, Byer dedicates her poem "Backwater" to Moira Bailis, with thanks for information she supplied concerning early Irish culture); and with other editors and writers of note. Moira offered them her words and thoughts, and frequently received personal, nongeneric replies — a very atypical experience compared to most American writers. She also wrote 17 short stories, two of which are pubished or forthcoming in *Sensations Magazine*.

"A job well done is its own reward," Moira shrewdly observes in "Cleaning House," one of the last poems in this collection. When taking a full-blown "collected works" approach to publishing, you take a risk — not every poem is necessarily a fully polished gem, and how to handle variations upon variations of individual poems is a challenge that has vexed numerous editors across the centuries. The approach here is to publish as much as possible, and to let each reader decide which individual poems or version of poems he or she prefers. It is my hope that, more often than not, you will find a great deal of talent, achievement, insight, wisdom, and beauty in her words. I am especially pleased to share this collection with her while she too is able to see, enjoy, and appreciate it.

To me, Moira Bailis is not just a fine poet and close personal friend — she has long been an example of graciousness, egalitarianism, and sincere encouragement and support of others in the New Jersey poetry scene. I was pleased to volunteer much of my spare time in 2010 to bring this project to completion, and view this endeavor as a way of saying "thank you" — on behalf of all who have interacted with her in poetry over these many decades — for creating a series of little observations and moments that add up to a comprehensive collection that speaks volumes about the world at large.

Let the world take note — and maybe learn to add a little travel to its personal itinerary.

— *David Messineo*
Thanksgiving 2010

<237>

ABOUT MOIRA BAILIS

OIRA BAILIS was born as "Moira Geraldine Moore" on February 26, 1921 in a large 18th Century Georgian house, in Athlone, County Westmeath, Ireland, to Andrew Moore and Gertrude Moore (*née* Higgins). As she relates in a hand-written autobiographical sketch, "It began ... In a big front bedroom in 'The Park,' Athlone, Co. Westmeath, Ireland. At that time, the Irish were fighting to get the British occupiers out of Ireland. Because of the situation, no doctor could come to my parents' house, so my mother had only the care and help of a nurse."[1] More details were gleaned from Moira by a New Jersey interviewer: "...a very pregnant mother, a nervous husband, a nurse, two servants, and two gun dogs awaited the arrival of the new baby the mother was about to deliver. As the guerillas and the British soldiers exchanged gunfire outside, the young father-to-be realized help was needed. So he broke the curfew, evaded the fighting, and walked into town to fetch the doctor. The laboring mother waited amid the sounds of guns pinging as the nearby combatants struggled. The dogs added to the uproar by whining and yowling incessantly. Young Moira's eventual arrival added just the right note of excitement."[2]

Moira was educated in private schools in Ireland. During WWII, while in Ireland, Moira spent most of her days at the Carnegie Library in Dún Laoghaire, reading and strengthening her background in literature, history, and the classics, and beginning what would become a life-long interest in self-education. She speaks five languages: English, Irish (Gaelic), German, Italian, and French.

Moira married filmmaker George Fleischmann in Dublin in 1947. In Dublin, she worked as a freelance journalist, starting with short documentary film scripts for Hibernia Films, along with articles for newspapers and magazines.

Her interest in travel took her to Switzerland and Austria in 1949 and 1950. She stayed with in-laws in Graz. Then, from 1952 to 1953, she lived in Rome, where she quickly learned Italian and, in turn, taught English to individuals.

In 1954, she lived in Cologne, Germany where, under the name "Moira Moore-Fleischmann" she was writing articles on German post-war reconstruction and other topics for the *Irish Independent* and for magazines. Moira met several writers and artists while living in Germany, including the future Nobel Prize winner Heinrich Böll. She arranged for him to visit

---

[1] Bailis, Moira. Autobiographical sketch, unpublished ms., dated June 29, 2008.
[2] Marshall, Pat. "An Irish poet in our midst!" Parishioner Profile column, *All Saints News*, Dec 1995/Jan 1996 (Leonia, NJ), p. 1.

<238>

Ireland, and in exchange, he arranged for her to have her own weekly radio show in Cologne, where she conducted journalism programs on Irish culture for *Nordwestdeutscher Rundfunk* (Northwest German Broadcasting -NWDR). One of the individuals she interviewed was the African-American novelist Ralph Ellison (*Invisible Man*). She also served as his personal tour guide during the German leg of his world tour.

In 1955 she lived in Munich, not far from a U.S. Army base ... "the most touching thing I saw were these two G.I.'s surrounded by children and they were giving the kids candy. It spoke a lot about the American character."[3]

In the summer of 1959, Moira was vacationing with her young son, Stefan, in a mountain inn near Innsbruck, Austria. The host of the inn asked Moira if she would mind being seated with an American tourist as he didn't speak German. Moira agreed. The American was a New York attorney named Jacob "Jack" Bailis. Although they soon returned to their respective homelands, they maintained a long-distance courtship. Her marriage to George Fleischmann having long faded, Moira obtained a divorce and subsequently married Jack in New York. Her family was completed with the arrival of her second son, Peter. Her marriage to Jack would be an enduring one, lasting until his sudden death in September, 2007.

Moira moved to the United States on July 15, 1963. The family lived for the next two-and-a-half years in upper Manhattan, off Broadway, adjacent to Fort Tryon Park. The park provided an opportunity for Moira to re-discover her creative talents, and she composed a number of watercolor paintings during this period.

On January 1, 1966, Moira and her family moved across the Hudson River to Fort Lee, New Jersey. At this point, she started volunteering in local schools to teach English to foreign students, before English as a Second Language courses were available. Her facility with languages enabled her to volunteer to teach English to Japanese, Greek, Hispanic, and Chinese children in Fort Lee Public School Number One.

According to another journalist, "The two things that impressed her the most in those first months were the enormous *amount* of volunteerism in America, and the awareness of the poor in America. . . . 'I was shocked that there were desperately poor people here. . . . I just wasn't prepared for the extreme poverty in Appalachia or on Indian reservations.'"[4] Moira got involved in several fronts of activism: visiting Indian reservations, joining the Quaker anti-war movement during the Vietnam war, joining the Cesar Chavez farm-worker movement (and having an opportunity to meet and

---

[3] Schmelter, Robert. "Romantic Irish spirit lives on in Moira Bailis" 'Local Poet' column, *Fort Lee Suburbanite*, April 28, 2006.
[4] Gressle, Gail. "Some things she did" in "A Gallery" column, published circa 1984.

<239>

talk with him personally), then protesting the growing nuclear threat. "She also volunteered her time and energy with the Irish Republican Club, a group that was for a non-sectarian Ireland; for the gradual development of uniting the whole of Ireland through political, social, and industrial means and not with arms."[5] Author Gail Gressle adds "I have joined hands with this 63-year-old woman to make a 'human chain for peace' across the George Washington Bridge."[6] Moira's husband Jack was a member of Lawyers' Committee on American Policy Towards Vietnam, and poems such as "Vietnam Christmas 1967," "Vietnam Christmas 1969," and "Indo-China" (June 26, 1972) stem from her impressions and experiences during that era. In 1971, Jack Bailis and the antiwar lawyers' group did a sit-in at the Capitol in Washington. He was arrested with them, and spent a night in jail, sharing his jail cell with famed child pediatrician Dr. Benjamin Spock.

While she had been an "occasional poet" since the age of eighteen, Moira focused even more of her energy into poetry and literature — and volunteer public service in those arts — starting in the 1980s. She began sending out works for publication circa 1988, and received her first notable publication credit (*Irish Voice* Poetry Contest, 2nd place in a contest with over 1,000 entries) in 1990. Several poetry awards followed in the 1990s and 2000s. Moira taught children's poetry workshops at Fort Lee Public Library starting around 1986 and for close to 20 years annually, as part of National Library Week, and also set up annual exhibits at the library on Irish culture and language around St. Patrick's Day.

Starting in the 1990s, Moira gave lectures on labor history at the Botto House/The American Labor Museum in Haledon. She also gave lectures on Irish culture and history at many places, including a class at Bergen Community College.

From 1996 to 2007, she was host of the Sunday morning radio show "The Poet's Corner" on WFDU-FM 89.1 (Fairleigh Dickinson Radio, Teaneck, NJ), sharing hosting duties with Dr. Leo Thorne (1996-circa 2001) and Okey Chenowith (circa 2002-2007). Throughout the 1990s and 2000s, she conducted poetry workshops and lectures, having "learned how to conduct poetry workshops from another writer, Lois Van Houten, ten years ago."[7] Lectures written by Moira on poets of various cultures (Chinese, Irish, Jewish, and Russian), and on individual poets (Akhmatova, Heaney, Joyce, Shakespeare, and more) have been found and documented among her papers.

Also starting in the 1990s, Moira joined several local poetry groups: The Saturday Afternoon Poets (Passaic), the North River Poets (Fort Lee),

---

[5] *Ibid.*

[6] *Ibid.*

[7] Nieves, Bianca A. "She's Devoted to Libraries." *The Bergen Record*, Wednesday, August 28, 1991. p. SE-2.

<240>

and the Main Street Poets (Fort Lee), where writing prompts by workshop leader Patrick Hammer, Jr. influenced the construction of many of the poems in this collection. She was an active member of the Bergen Poets, the New Jersey Poetry Society, the League of Minnesota Poets, and took part in many of the public and private readings held by *Sensations Magazine* from 1992 to present. Also during this decade, she began her long-term writer/editor relationships with three literary magazine publisher/editors: Melanie Pimont (*North River Review*), Carole Heffley (*Feelings Poetry Magazine*), and David Messineo (*Sensations Magazine*), all of whom have published her work prominently and frequently (the Publication Credits section in both volumes details these and other publication credits). In 2003, Moira teamed up with Ana Doina to prepare and publish *poems*, a chapbook containing 46 of Moira's poems. Moira also wrote the foreword to one published poetry book: *A Dusting of Star Fall: Love Poems* by Sal Buttaci.

A core component of Moira's life has been to help and bring attention to others, even in small ways. Moira was one of two individuals to help get a plaque installed at the homestead of writer Elizabeth Bowen in Ireland. In 2003, while taking one of her many walks through Fort Lee, she rediscovered the grave of a forgotten Civil War soldier, James Conway (subject of her poem "Hero") at Madonna Cemetery. She brought it to the attention of a local VFW post in Fort Lee, and the grave was subsequently marked and rededicated. She also supported many animal rights groups.

In a handwritten biographical note, Moira mentions that her favorite poets include Keats, Yeats, Hardy, Edward Thomas, Longfellow, Frost, Mary Oliver, Carruth, Donald Hall, Heaney, and Joan McBreen. She is frequently quoted in articles which can be found about her online, discussing her passions for libraries, books, poetry, volunteerism, and the importance of helping and supporting others, especially those in need.

Moira has two sons, Stefan and Peter, and one grandson, Jacob. Moira still resides in Fort Lee, New Jersey, in the home she and her family moved into on January 1, 1966, making her a Fort Lee resident for 45 years. She turned 90 on February 26, 2011.

<241>

THE TRAVELS OF MOIRA BAILIS, 1921-2011

Compiled by Stefan Bailis

1921	Born Athlone, Co. Westmeath.
1927	Moved with family to Dalkey, Co. Dublin.
1929	Tutored at home.
1930	Attended same school that Mother Teresa taught in (at a different time)
1932	Went to Mount Annville private boarding school, in Dundrum.
1937	Went to stay with Aunt Tess, England, for the summer.
1938	Went to Leeson Street School. Completed high school.
1945	Attended Trinity College, part time — several classes.
1947	Married George Fleischmann, moved to Dublin.
1949	Visited Switzerland and Austria, stayed with brother-in-law in Graz.
1950	Visited Switzerland and Austria.
1952	Moved to Rome. Taught English while learning Italian.
1953	Returned to Ireland.
1954	Moved to Cologne. Flew to Amsterdam. Train to Cologne. Returned via Paris later that year.
1955	Moved to Munich in about January, returned in about July.
1958	Visited west coast of Ireland; stayed with Heinrich Böll (1972 Nobel Prize for Literature).
1959	Visited Switzerland and Austria. Met Jacob Bailis in the Alps.
1960	Visited Cornwall, England.
1963	Visited New York. Married on St. Patrick's Day to Jacob Bailis.
1963	Emigrated to USA, arriving in New York City on July 15.
1964	Visited Ireland for the summer.
1965	Visited Ireland for the summer.
1966	No long trips this year. Her mother, instead, visited Fort Lee for a month in September.
1967	Visited Ireland for the summer.

<242>

1968   Visited Canada; also trip to Virginia with other states along the way.

1969   Visited Ireland for three weeks that summer; also visited Massachusetts for a couple of weeks.

1970   Visited Canada via New England.

1971   Visited Canada via New England.

1972   Visited Ireland for the summer.

1974   Visited Ireland for the summer.

1975   Visited New Orleans?

1979   She flew west to San Francisco to Sydney via Hawaii. Then on to Perth. Stayed there about a month. Flew back to New York via India and London. Also visited Miami, Florida this year.

1980s   In the 1980s through the early 1990s, she made many trips to upstate New York with Jack, mostly to Boonville.

1980   Visited Miami, Florida.

1982   Visited Ireland, possibly.

1985   Visited Ireland.

1986   Visited Ireland.

1987   Visited Ireland for funeral of mother.

1988   Visited Ireland for funeral of brother, Jim.

1992   Visited Ireland.

1993   Visited Minnesota.

1994   Visited Ireland and Cornwall, England again (last trip there was in 1960).

1996   Visited Ireland.

1998   Visited Ireland.

1999   Visited Arizona.

2002   May have visited Minnesota this year.

2009   Visited Pennsylvania — Bar Mitzvah of Grant Meserve, most recent out-of-state travel.

<243>

PUBLICATION CREDITS — AMERICA AND IRELAND

At the end of 2010, Moira Bailis has between 200 to 225 poetry publication credits, as outlined below. She wishes to thank the editors and publishers of the following publications, past and present, for sharing her writings with their audiences during the 1990s, 2000s, and 2010s.

Editor's Note: For each listing, poems are listed in alphabetic order by title. Poems labeled "unverified at press time" may be poems submitted and published, or poems submitted but not selected for publication. This section should be viewed as a work in progress, and we welcome feedback from those who can verify any partial or missing information.

POEMS PUBLISHED IN JOURNALS, LITERARY MAGAZINES, NEWSLETTERS, AND NEWSPAPERS

Appalachian Journal (1 poem, verified)
    Volume 30, No. 1, Fall 2002, p. 124.
        "The Museum at Cullowhee"
The Black River Journal (5 poems, all verified)
    December 2001, p. 16.
        "Autumn Rapture"
    February/March 2002, p. 9.
        "Hiking the Columbia Trail"
    Spring 2002, p. 23
        "A Peaceful Place"
    Holiday/Early Winter 2002/03, p. 22.
        "A Jersey Welcome"
    Spring/Summer 2003, p. 14.
        "The Source"
BP Links (Quarterly Newsletter of Bergen Poets) (9 poems, 5 verified)
    Vol. 1, 1999 (unverified at press time)
        "Oracle," "The Farm at Derry," "Upstate"
    Vol. 1, Issue 2, 1999, p. 4.
        "The Holiness of Fall," "Mending Glass"
    Vol. 2, Issue 4, Fall 2000
        "It Has to Do With Seeing," "Memento," "Sonas"
    2001 (claimed/unverified at press time)
        "Rain"

The Contemporary Review, Iowa (6 poems, all verified)
    January 2001

<244>

"It Has to Do With Seeing," "Sonas," "The Farm at Derry"
July 2001, pp. 4-6.
"Courtesy," "The Bike," "The Lions of Rome"

Dalkey Community Council Newsletter (Ireland) (4 poems, 2 verified)
1995 (unverified at press time)
"Berrying" (aka "Brambles in Ireland"), "Feral," "Heartland"
September 1995, No. 235, p. 9.
"Feral"
October 2004, No. 336, Vol. 1., p. 23.
"Autumn Rapture"

Defined Providence (1 poem, verified)
Vol. 6, 1998, p. 42.
"Upstate"

Feelings Poetry Magazine (8 poems, 6 verified)
1992 (unverified at press time)
"After Rain"
Vol. 4, No. 3, Spring 1993, p. 23.
"Rained Out Boulevard"
Vol. 5, No. 2, Winter 1993, p. 11.
"Sales Pitch"
Vol. 6, No. 1., Fall 1994, p. 34.
"Oil Eater"
Vol. 7, No. 1, Autumn 1995, p. 20.
"The Farm at Derry"
Vol. 7, No. 2, Winter 1996, p. 39.
"Winter Comfort"
Vol. 7, No. 6, p. 6.
"The Source"
Spring 1997 (unverified at press time)
"Rain"

Irish Voice (1 poem, verified)
Sat Nov 24, 1990, p. 21.
"Brambles" (aka "Brambles in Ireland")
Second Place in contest with over 1,000 entries.
Earliest known poetry publication credit.

Journal of Irish Literature (1 poem, verified)
Vol. XXII, No. 3, September 1993 (Last Issue), p. 111.
"On Seeing Maud Gonne"

<245>

The Moccasin (League of Minnesota Poets) (25 poems, all verified)
  Vol. LVII, 1994, p. 42.
    "Coming Into the Heartland By Air"
  Vol. LVIII, 1995, pp. 15 & 23.
    "August," "Broken Blossoms"
  Vol. LIX, 1996, pp. 10, 11 & 43.
    "A gentle spring breeze" (Haiku), "Rained Out Boulevard,"
      "Winter Gothic"
  Vol. LX, 1997, pp. 21 & 45.
    "Advent," "Rain"
  Vol. LXI, 1998, pp. 15 & 28.
    "He Says," "Patronymic"
  Vol. LXII, 1999, pp. 28 & 31.
    "Father" (aka "Forecast"), "Summer Heat"
  Vol. LXIII, 2000, p. 28.
    "Oil Eater"
  Vol. LXIV, 2001, pp. 26, 31 & 37.
    "Elegy for a Brother" (aka "Oracle"), "Rainstorm," "Williams
      Country" (aka "Memento")
  Vol. LXV, 2002, pp. 26 & 35.
    "Brambles in Ireland," "Diner"
  Vol. LXVI, 2003, pp. 17, 21, 27 & 35.
    "A whisper of wind" (Haiku), "Remember," "Sun behind
      dark clouds" (Haiku), "The Bike"
  Vol. LXVII, 2004, pp. 14 & 18.
    "Haiku," "Teddy"
  Vol. LXVIII, 2005, p. 34.
    "Hearing Brodsky Read, Dublin, 1992"

New Hibernia Review (8 poems, all verified)
  Vol. 9:2, Summer 2005, pp. 42-59.
    "Allta," "Burning Coal," "Company Manners," "Heartland,"
      "Memento," "The Museum at Cullowhee,"
      "Patrick Kavanagh on Pembroke Road,"
      "Three Rock Mountain"

NJ Conservation Foundation (1 poem, unverified at press time)
  1995
    "Highlands"

Nimrod (1 poem, unverified at press time)
  2001
        "Ancestors"

<246>

North River Review (35 poems, all verified)
    Issue 1, Spring 1992, pp. 8, 10, 15, 17.
        "Alone in the Cemetery," "Diner" (aka "At the Diner"),
        "Passage at Overpeck," "Stiles"
    Issue 2, Fall/Winter 1992, pp. 10, 18, 21, 25, 34.
        "Consanguinity," "For Emily Brontë," "He Says,"
        "The Holiness of Fall," "The Source"
    Issue 3, 1993, pp. 1, 4, 8, 15, 24, 28, 37.
        "Confusion," "Early Morning Encounter with the Entomologist,"
        "Just Like Jane," "Light Touch," "Medieval,"
        "Mending Glass," "Rosebud"
    Issue 4, 1994, pp. 2, 9, 17, 26, 31.
        "At the Bay," "Hearing Brodsky Read, Dublin, 1992"
        (aka "Brodsky Reads"), "Patronymic," "The Farm
        at Derry, N.H., 1991," "Wir hatten uns Gefürchtet..."
    Issue 5, 1995, pp. 3, 7, 15, 17.
        "Allta," "Miss Holybrooke in Central Park," "On Seeing
        Maud Gonne, Dublin, 1944," "Sonas"
    Issue 6, 1996, pp. 2, 8, 11.
        "Four Haiku," "In China," "Upstate"
    Issue 7, 1997, pp. 6, 27.
        "Highlands," "Masterpiece"
    Issue 8, 1998, pp. 8, 32.
        "Conspiracy," "Memento"

Parnassus Literary Journal (18 poems, 13 verified)
    1997 (unverified at press time)
        "Nice Day"
    1998 or 1999 (claimed/unverified at press time)
        "Just Like Jane"
    Vol. 22, No. 2, Summer 1998, p. 79.
        "Discretion"
    Vol. 23, No. 1, Spring 1999, p. 54.
        "After Rain"
    Vol. 23, No 3, Fall/Winter 1999, p. 27
        "A is for Aardvark"
    Vol. 24, No. 1, Spring 2000, p. 11.
        "Sol"
    Vol. 25, No. 2, Summer 2001, p. 49.
        "Lightweight, as in Superficial"
    Vol. 25, No. 3, Fall/Winter 2001, p. 31.
        "Diner" (aka "At the Diner")
    Vol. 26, No. 1, Spring 2002, p. 5

<247>

"Sales Pitch"
Vol. 26, 2003 (claimed/unverified at press time)
  "Brambles in Ireland," "Voice Mail"
Vol. 27, No. 2, Summer 2003, p. 15.
  "Poetry Class"
Vol. 27, No. 3, Fall/Winter 2003, p. 6.
  "Autumn Rapture"
Vol. 28, No. 1, Spring 2004, pp. 67-68.
  "Stiles," "The Bike"
Vol. 28, No. 2, Summer 2004, p. 73.
  "Aftermath"
Vol. 29, No. 1, Spring 2005, p. 61.
  "Where Is My Father?"
Vol. 29, No. 2, Autumn 2005, p. 31.
  "Bird and the Sea"

Poet Magazine (3 poems, 1 verified)
  Vol. 4, No. 3, Winter 1992-1993, p. 17.
    "Brambles in Ireland"
  1994 (claimed/unverified at press time)
    "Just Like Jane," "Mending Glass"

Poetry Forum Journal (5 poems, all verified)
  1991 (One of six contest winners)
    "Irish September"
  March 1993, p. 13.
  "Rosebud"
  Fall 1993, p. 15.
    "A Small Remembrance"
  1994
    "Budtime"
  Fall 1995, p. 13
    "Native" (aka "Native American")

Pralaton (1 poem, verified)
  No. 17, August 2006, pp. 21-22.
    "Just Like Jane"

Quabbin Voices: The Friends of Quabbin Newsletter (2 poems,
  both verified)
  Vol. 7, No. 4, p. 5.
    "Landfall," "Quabbin"

<248>

Sensations Magazine (30 poems, 2 stories, 1 book review, all verified)
   Issue 8, Fall 1992, p. 36.
      "Reds"
   Issue 9, 1993, p. 44.
      "Bird and the Sea"
   Issue 10, Summer 1994, p. 12.
      "Mississippi Death Trip
   Issue 11, Winter 1994-1995, p. 53.
      "Dreamers"
   Issue 12, 1995, inside back cover w/full color photography.
      "Mr. Meyer at Coney Island"
   Issue 13, 1996, p. 29.
      "French Nails"
   Issue 14, Spring 1997, p. 82.
      "Heritage" (also "The Atheist" — fiction by Moira Bailis)
   Issue 16, Fall 1997, p. 23.
      "Happiness" (aka "Sonas")
   Issue 17, Winter 1997, p. 38.
      "Miss Holybrooke in Central Park"
   Issue 38, Spring 2005, pp. 86-87.
      Critical review of *poems* by Moira Bailis (2003 chapbook).
   Issue 40, 2006, p. 229 & p. 263.
      "Imagining the Future," "Three Rock Mountain"
   Issue 42, Fall/Winter 2007, p. 296 & p. 313.
      "On Seeing Maud Gonne, Dublin, 1942" and "Sonas"
         (republished in memory of Jack Bailis)
   Issue 44, Fall/Winter 2008, pp. 14-15, w/full color photography.
      "Dreamers" (republished from Issue 11)
   Issue 46, Fall/Winter 2009, p. 30.
      "In Emily's Garden"
   Issue 47, Spring/Summer 2010, p. 26 & p. 70.
      "Rap," "The Two Swans"
   Issue 48, Fall/Winter 2010, p. 24, 41, 45, 64 & 67.
      "Aftermath," "August 2005 - Riegelsville, PA," "In the Republic
         of Caring," "Sol," "Summer Heat"
Sensations Magazine Supplement 3, "American Presidents,"
   Spring 2011
   "JFK"
Sensations Magazine Silver Anniversary Fiction Issue 49,
   Winter 2011, accepted/publication coming.
   "A Fearful Child" (fiction)
      Sensations Magazine Silver Anniversary Poetry Issue 49,
         Winter 2011, accepted/publication coming.

<249>

"A House with No Key," "Alignment," "Antietam,"
"Autumn Again," "Coming from Fort Worth,"
"Wir hatten uns Gefürchtet..."
Sensations Magazine Issue 50, *Titanic* (Final Issue), Spring 2012,
accepted/publication coming.
"Titanic at Belfast"

Westmeath Chronicle (Ireland) (1 poem, unverified)
"Revenant"

POEMS PUBLISHED IN ANTHOLOGIES

Anderie Poetry Press Anthologies (3 poems, 2 verified)
1994 *Songs of Glory* Anthology, p. 42.
"Winter Gothic"
1995 *How Do I Love Thee* Anthology, p. 103.
"Sonas"
1996 *Womankind: The Poetry of Women* Anthology
"He Says"

Bergen Poets Anthologies (6 poems, all verified)
30th Anniversary Anthology, 1999, pp. 12-13.
"Flying into the Heartland," "Where Is My Father?"
No. 13, 2000, pp. 28-29.
"The Lions of Rome," "Rain"
No. 14, 2002, pp. 30-31.
"Aftermath," "Passage at Overpeck"
The Best of Feelings (1 poem, verified)
1994, p. 25.
"Miss Holybrooke in Central Park"

Friends for Life Poetry Anthology 2007 (2 poems, both verified)
"Heartland," "Aftermath" (unpaginated anthology)

Lovelines — Poems of Love and Loss (4 poems, all verified)
1995 - p. 6, 15, 28 & 31.
"Dalkey," "Rained-Out Boulevard," "Shadow of a Rose,"
"Where Is My Father?"

Main Street Poets & Writers Anthologies (32 poems, 31 verified)
Vol. 1, 1998 (unverified at press time)
"Tea Party"
Vol. 4, 2000, pp. 18-21.

<250>

"After Rain," "Discretion," "Rain," "Sales Pitch"
"Blue Cover" edition, undated (likely 1999 or 2001), pp. 42-48.
 "Broken Blossoms," "Firs in Snow," "It Has to Do with Seeing,"
  "Just Like Jane," "Roan Inish."
Vol. 6, 2004, pp. 36-40.
 "Aftermath," "Autumn Rapture," "In Emily's Garden," "Mending
  Glass," "Poetry Class," "The Farm at Derry," "Three Rock
  Mountain"
Vol. 7, 2005, pp. 58-59.
 "Bird and the Sea," "In Ogdensburg," "Jersey Day,"
  "Passage at Overpeck"
Vol. 8, 2006
 "Alone in the Cemetery," "Brambles in Ireland," "Diner"
  (aka "At the Diner"), "Nice Day!", "Proper Manners,"
  "The Bike," "The Lions of Rome"
Vol. 9, 2007
 "Four Haiku," "The Paulinskill Valley Trail Sussex 6,"
  "The Secret" (aka "Ceircin"), "Upstate"

New Jersey Poetry Society, Inc. Anthologies (9 poems, all verified)
1995 Anthology
edge of sounds, pp. 6-9.
 "Brambles in Ireland," "Hearing Brodsky Read,"
  "Mending Glass," "Sonas," "The Holiness of Fall,"
  "The Source"
2003 Anthology
Road to Recovery, A Tribute to 9/11 and Other Poems, p. 57.
 "Aftermath" (First Place Winner, Spring/Summer 2002 contest)

2004 Anthology
"Seeds of April's Sowing" Poems, p. 1.
 "After Rain," "Shadow of a Rose"

<251>

PUBLISHED ARTICLES ON WRITERS (4, all verified)

Hamburger Anzeiger, October 11, 1954, p. 8.
    "In leicht singendem Tönfall: Ralph Ellison in Deutschland"
    Byline: Moira Fleischmann-Moore.

Feelings Poetry Journal, Fall 1996, pp. 7-8.
    "Out of Ireland: The Poetry of Seamus Heaney, Nobel
        Prize 1996"

Feelings Poetry Journal, Spring 1997, p. 4.
    "Joycevoice: The Poetry of James Joyce"

Feelings Poetry Journal, Vol. 8, No. 4, Summer/Fall 1997, pp. 12-13.
    "Heartbreak & Heroism: Anna Akhmatova"

OTHER PUBLISHED ARTICLES

Dalkey Community Council Newsletter
    September 1994, No. 191, pp. 5-6.
    "Memories of Dalkey"

<252>

POEM TITLES EXCLUDED
FROM THIS COMPILATION

"Trust," written pre-1989 — not located by press time.

"Lines to a Tom Cat," referred to as published in *Cats Magazine* in Florida — not located by press time.

"Poet" For David M. Written circa 1992-93 — not located by press time.

"Melody," "New Jersey, My State," "The Sound of Happiness" — need work.

"What Purpose Music," "On Opening a Map of Ireland," "New Windsor Settlement 1783" — incomplete fragments.

<253>

ABOUT THE EDITOR

DAVID MESSINEO is the Publisher of *Sensations Magazine* (www.sensationsmag.com), a rare three-consecutive-year winner in the national American Literary Magazine Awards (including two First Place Awards, in 1994 and 1996). The author of six published poetry books, he has been an active fixture and influence in the New Jersey poetry scene since 1987, and a poetry editor since 1979. He was one of 26 individuals statewide to be honored with a 2009 New Jersey State Jefferson Award for Public Service for his research, publishing, and public programming efforts for both *Sensations Magazine* and its current parent company, The Six Centuries Club. He was a contributing editor to *A Funny Thing Happened on the Way to the Interview* by Gregory E. Farrell (Gillette, NJ: Edin Books, Inc., 1996), and one of five editors for *Beyond the Rift: Poets of the Palisades* (Providence, RI: The Poet's Press, 2010). David volunteered much of his spare personal time during 2010 to find, type, collect, and sequence this two-volume set of collected poems by Moira Bailis, in honor of their continuing writer/editor relationship, and twenty years of their personal friendship. This is his first effort at compiling a sweeping, comprehensive "life's work" collection for an individual poet.

<255>

ABOUT THIS BOOK

THE BODY TYPE for this book is ITC Cheltenham, a 1975 redesign by Tony Stan of an Oldstyle serif type originally designed in 1896 by Bertram Goodhue and Ingalls Kimball for The Cheltenham Press. Immensely popular in the 1920s and 1930s, the typeface is still used by *The New York Times*. In the early days of phototypesetting, Cheltenham was deprecated by many designers as a "hot metal" face associated with newspapers and "yellow journalism." Today it is appreciated for its visual charm and high legibility. Notes and bibliographical information at the back of the book are set in Aldine, a face inspired by the designs of the great Venetian humanist publisher and printer Aldus Manutius.

Block initials are a Poet's Press adaptation of an alphabet created for The Chiswick Press. Section titles are set in Morris Troy, a typeface designed by William Morris for the Kelmscott Press.

The cover art is based on a photograph by Tom Fitzpatrick, who provides this narrative and background on the locale: "The statues from Boa Island in County Fermanagh had made a lasting impression on me. The name *Boa* comes from *Badhbha*, war goddess of the Ulster Celts. This area remained the center of the Druidic cult long after Christianity had arrived in Ireland. The 'Janus' figure has a hollow (a deep libation stoup) between the heads which may have held sacrificial blood. The smaller 'Lusty Man' was originally from nearby Lustymore Island, hence the name. The Ulster-born poet William Allingham (1824-89) commented:

> *Up the airy mountain,*
> *Down the rushy glen,*
> *We daren't go a-hunting,*
> *For fear of little men.*

This half-forgotten graveyard is difficult to find and access. We had to ignore 'No Trespassing' signs, walk down a farmer's road, climb over a gate and go through a field to see these little men. It was worth the effort."

The portrait of Moira Bailis is a photograph by Stefan Bailis.

<257>

www.ingramcontent.com/pod-product-compliance
Lightning Source LLC
Chambersburg PA
CBHW021502090426
42739CB00007B/429